Soothe

your
mind-body-spirit
guide for dealing with
crappy
emotions

Less stress.
More resilience.
Starting now.

heidi kopacek, PsyD, LP, RYT

Published by:
PESI Publishing & Media
PESI, Inc
3839 White Ave.
Eau Claire, WI 54703

Editing: Deb Burdick
Layout: Bookmasters & Amy Rubenzer
Cover: Amy Rubenzer

ISBN: 9781683732327

ABOUT THE AUTHOR

Heidi Kopacek, PsyD, LP, RYT, is a licensed psychologist who practices a holistic approach to emotional health. Her integrative mind-body-spirit therapy focuses on soothing and healing the body, challenging the fear of the mind, and helping her clients live in a way that wakes up their deeper sense of joy and purpose in life. Dr. Kopacek is trained in mindfulness and meditation, nutritional interventions for anxiety and depression, breathing techniques, and body awareness. She is also a certified yoga instructor who teaches yoga designed specifically for emotional health.

DEDICATION

To my parents Ted and Cindy. Thank you for being my biggest cheerleaders. And for always sending me home with leftovers.

CONTENTS

INTRODUCTION:
WHAT IS THIS HERE BOOK ABOUT?

Emotions. They shape every moment of our human experience. Everything we do, every single day, is driven by how we *feel*. Our emotions are what make us human. What we live for. And yet, at the end of the day, do we really know what they are? Do we know where our emotions come from? Why we have them? And what the bejiminy we *do* with them? Shockingly, although emotions are at the very core of our being, they are still pretty much a total mystery to us.

As a psychologist, I see this every day—all of us are confused about even the most basic aspects of our emotional experiences. We wonder what's normal and what's not. We feel ashamed for having negative emotions. We believe everyone else must have learned some elusive formula for happiness on the one day of a class we missed.

I too, even after earning an advanced degree in psychology, found myself confused about the *basics of emotions*. No textbook or professor really explained in a satisfying way what emotions *were*. And my clients were confused as well. Did they have some sort of genetic disorder causing them to experience negative moods? Or were they just not thinking positively enough? Or were they doomed to experience negative emotions as a result of unresolved childhood issues? And was everyone else magically positive, healthy and happy?

Over time, and through my exploration with clients, I began to form a theory and approach to emotions that helped make sense of emotions, why we have them, and *how to tend to the crappy ones in a way that actually helped*. As I became more skilled in teaching this theory of emotions, exciting things began to happen in therapy. Negative emotions started to have less of a stranglehold on clients' lives. They understood where their emotions were coming from and could more skillfully attend to the core source of those emotions. They became less overwhelmed by or ashamed of their negative emotions. They figured out meaningful ways to soften negative emotions rather than haphazardly trying to distract from them or shove them down. And most importantly, they could see more vividly what needed to happen in their lives to generate more positive, vibrant and yummy emotions.

Understanding emotions is a game changer.

When we know what emotions are, we can witness our experiences with newfound clarity. When we know the evolutionary purpose of anger, anxiety and depression, we can wisely dialogue with our emotions and appreciate how they are trying to help us. And when we have a universal formula for tending to emotional experience, we are empowered and emboldened to attend to any, and I mean *any*, situation with resilience. In short, the key to alleviating negative emotions is to *understand* them.

Hello and welcome to my book. My name is Dr. Heidi Kopacek (sigh—I wish my parents had named me something more interesting, like "Ninja" or "Velveeta"). I am a licensed psychologist who explores emotional well-being from a holistic perspective. Said another way, I am a psychologist who works with the well-being of the body, the mind, and the spirit.

Now to be fair, unlike some authors of self-help books, I do not have an inspiring story of overcoming extreme drama and pain. Every human experiences challenges and difficulty, but I have been deeply humbled in my profession to see the intensity of hardship experienced and surmounted by some. However, like all of us, I am no stranger to crappy emotions—though on the surface of things you might not see it.

My childhood was relatively stable, if somewhat predictable. I grew up in the suburbs of Minneapolis. I was that annoying student who raised her hand too much and sidled up to the teachers. My friends were the type of kids all parents wanted for their own child. I spent crammed weekends engaged in resume-building extracurricular activities. I received hearty doses of validation from my family, my teachers, my community. I went to college like I was supposed to (although the grades dropped, the friends became more controversial, and the extracurriculars were no longer appropriate for the resume).

After college, an insatiable hunger for life burst from within (maybe it was all the cafeteria carbs). With a ferocity that would drive small pets under the sofa, I decided to travel the world. I took a crash course on how to teach English and spent my 20s jumping from one country to the next. Between teaching contracts, I whisked off to Alaska and spent summers hiking, kayaking and cobbling together a living. I had freedom. I had adventure. I could proudly fit all my possessions into a single backpack. The world was mine! *But my emotions were not. They were all over the place, and only rarely positive.*

If you had asked, I would have told you I was happy and that I liked my life. And that would not have been a lie. But there were also these, I'm not quite sure how to describe them, *undercurrents.* I loved my life, but I was also constantly doubting, questioning, managing stress and trying to figure out the future. These undercurrents were experienced in the form of wheel-spinning voices lurking just below the level of consciousness. These voices said things like, "What in the world do I want to be when I grow up? What's wrong with me that I'm single? How come I'm not making any money while others are earning great salaries? How do I figure out my purpose in life? Why can't I be more disciplined and productive? How come I never know the right thing to say or do socially? Where did everyone else learn what to say or do socially? And how, how, *how* does everyone else manage to have a good hair day *every friggin' day?*"

Then, at the age of 30, I decided it was time to become a grown-up. I took a job in the for-profit world, inhaled the fluorescent lighting of cubicle life, and started proudly throwing around adult-ish words like "bandwidth" and "W-2 forms." I worked hard, enjoyed happy hours with friends, experienced love (and some things that I thought were love, but in retrospect I must have eaten some bad sauerkraut with hallucinogenic properties). In any case, I was a woman with a home, a career, a latte fetish and a collection of cute shoes that did *not* fit into a single backpack—thank you very much. I had arrived! *But my emotions had not. They were all over the place and only rarely positive. What the fire truck??*

Yet again, had you asked, I would have told you I was happy and I liked my life. And this would have been true. But gosh-dangity there still were those same undercurrents. No matter what I did, my mind kept spinning with those same tiresome thoughts. "You still aren't earning enough money. You are not interesting enough. You're not important enough. You are not pretty enough. You are not driven and directed enough. Your house is not updated enough. Your calendar is not full enough. You are not doing enough with your life. You. Are. Not. Enough."

I think everyone can relate to my "undercurrents" in their own way. As humans, we generally like life and want to be alive, and yet we equally find life to be exhausting and stressful. Sometimes the challenges we experience are visible to others (like the time I tried to prepare an American meal of hamburgers for my German host family … *in the microwave*). But oftentimes, our crappy emotions are experienced as hazy background noise. They're the spinning thoughts in the back of our minds that others can't see or observe.

All in all, many of us are doing okay keeping up with life. Some of us actually look like we're killing it. But we're not feeling all that great moment to moment and we're not sure what to do about it. There's a voice deep inside of us that says, "You should do more, be more, have more than you do, you dumb donkey." In the words of a born-and-raised Minnesotan: Uffda!

Soothe: Your Mind-Body-Spirit Guide for Dealing with Crappy Emotions will answer, hopefully in a fun-to-read and accessible way, the questions of: What are emotions? Why do we have them? And most importantly: What, what, WHAT are we supposed to do with the ones we don't like?

This book outlines how to expertly tend to emotions physically, mentally and spiritually. It will provide you with the knowledge and confidence to navigate every negative emotional experience life can throw at you. *Yes, every single emotional experience*, ranging from niggling worry about how your butt looks in those jeans, to irritation about that inflated coworker who never shuts up, to dealing with the February winter "blahs," to obsessing about finances and debt, to recovering from a broken heart, to managing angst about the future of the world, to navigating a society that judges or mistreats you, to dealing with illness or aging, to grieving the loss of a loved one and even to healing from abuse or trauma. *That is the power of understanding emotions.*

So roll up your sleeves, slap your hands together and get ready. It is my sincere hope that, by the end of these 159 pages, you will experience an exhilarating sense of, "Ah-ha! I get it! I get these emotion thingies." You will possess a cornucopia of strategies for easing and soothing challenging emotional experiences. And you will become inspired to live a life that cultivates and nurtures vital and juicy emotional experiences.

Are you ready? It's time to begin!

CHAPTER 1

■ ■ ■

SERIOUSLY, WHAT IS AN EMOTION ANYWAY?

Obviously we all know what emotions are to an extent. But stop and think about this for a moment. What is an emotion really? If an alien abducted you and said, "Define *emotion* or we're going to give you a wedgie!" would you have a response?

Most of us know that an emotion is a feeling. And most of us would agree that we like good feelings and we don't like crappy ones. Some more scientific types might explain that emotions are chemical combinations of hormones and neurotransmitters generated in response to a stimulus. Merriam-Webster's dictionary says that emotions are: 1) the affective aspect of consciousness; 2) a state of feeling; 3) a conscious mental reaction (such as anger or fear) subjectively experienced as strong feeling usually directed toward a specific object and typically accompanied by physiological and behavioral changes in the body.

I don't know about you, but those definitions don't help me one single bit. They don't explain where emotions come from or why we have them, let alone what in the heck we're supposed to do with them. I have even found that men and women with degrees in psychology are hard-pressed to explain emotions in a truly effective way.

Let's change that. For this book, we're going to use the following definition of an emotion: *An emotion is an experience, thought, or belief expressed in your body.*

Let me repeat this, because it's important. An emotion is an experience, thought, or belief expressed in your body.

1

Think about this for a moment. How do you know when you're having an emotion? You *feel* it. What do you feel an emotion with? Your body. If you are on a roller coaster and feel a rush of excitement in your stomach, that is an *experience expressed in your body*. If you are running late and thinking about how irked your boss is going to be, that tightening chest and shortened breath is a *thought expressed in your body*. If you believe that the world is ultimately beautiful and the awareness of this softens your shoulders and causes you to exhale, that is *a belief expressed in your body*.

By the way, if you're wondering what the difference is between a thought and a belief, we'll get to that later, I promise. For now, know that an emotion is an experience, thought, or belief expressed in your body. Yes, I've snuck in that definition three times now, but rest assured, if you are abducted by aliens and forced to answer this question under threat of a wedgie, you will be safe!

CULTURE AND EMOTION

I'm guessing few will debate me if I argue that our collective culture has conflicted and confusing views of emotions. As a society, we don't directly address or tend to our emotions in an organized way. We cultivate intellect through our educational system. We address behavior with our system of laws, rules, policies, and regulations. We explore values through our spiritual and political institutions. We support physical health with hospitals, doctors, and managed health care.

But where, exactly, do we as a society collectively address emotions? We just plain don't. Yes, we have counselors and psychologists who can help us talk about our feelings, but aren't these mostly for the "really crazy" people? And yes, we have a field of study called psychology, but we all know that the ones who go into that profession are bazoinkers themselves, right? And yes, there are an abundance of emotional self-help books that tell us vague things like, "feel your emotions," and it's "okay to feel." But, at the end of the day, we are left with the sense that taking time and truly learning about emotions is either a waste of time or a fruitless task.

In our culture, as a general rule, emotions either leak out in increments or build up and burst forth now and again. We might tear up, but we take a deep breath and tuck the tears back in. We might bite our cheeks in irritation, but we don't do anything until that irritation either mounts into something more explosive or turns inward and becomes illness or depression. We might feel happy when good fortune comes our way, but only in certain socially condoned conditions are we allowed to yelp, dance, or celebrate without restraint. This is especially true if, like me, you grew up in the Midwest where stoicism is the gold standard of emotional health. Conversely, if someone releases feelings in an uncomfortable or public way, we call them "emotional" which is code for "keep your distance."

Though there are variations from culture to culture on the appropriateness of emotions and to what degree they may be expressed, collectively we seem to agree on one universal rule and it goes something like this: Imagine, for a moment, that a very important representative from our National Department of Homeland Emotional Health (I know that's not a real thing, but it would be cool if it were) takes the pulpit at a press conference, clears his throat authoritatively and officially announces the following:

"Ladies and Gentlemen. We've taken a formal vote and decided to overturn our former proclamation that boys aren't allowed to cry. They are now allowed to cry. However, all other standards have remained the same. Feelings are to be experienced in private.

If we are going to experience them collectively, it must be done at sports events, musical concerts, and Black Friday shopping extravaganzas. On all other occasions, if you decide to feel your feelings, please do not inconvenience others or make them uncomfortable with those feelings. And please experience your feelings quietly, not loudly. And do not discuss them at length or examine them too deeply.

Oh, and please do not use feelings in your decision making or life planning. And again, please don't forget that part about not inconveniencing others or making them uncomfortable with your emotions … ."

Now I know that was oversimplified and silly, and yet? As a culture, it's not hard to see that we value logic, intellect, professionalism, objectivity. And how are all of those defined? *By the absence of emotion.* We live in a world where the standard for wellness means feelings are perceived to be under control.

But there's a huge problem here. And by huge, I mean behemoth, NFL-football-player, prom-night-pimple HUGE. And the problem is this: Logic and intellect are important for navigating the outer world, but they are useless for aiding our inner one. Logic and intellect can help us solve problems, build groovy things, and figure out what needs to get done in a day, but they don't do a darn thing for establishing connections with others, helping with matters of the heart, or cultivating vitality.

Facts and data are the building blocks of our outer world, but emotions are the guiding lights of our inner one. Emotions provide us with crucial information about the experiences and needs of our bodies, our minds, and our spirits. Emotions give us clues about the decisions that are right for us and the boundaries that we need to set in life. But more on that later.

For now, it is important to note that emotions *are* a form of logic. They are the logic of our inner experience. They have rules and an order and a purpose, but these rules only make sense to the heart, not the mind. Emotions are not just random experiences to be stifled or overcome or dismissed. They are sources of information to be weighed and considered. And the purpose of this book is to clarify how emotions work, what they are trying to say, and how to best engage with them.

CHAPTER 2

WHERE DO EMOTIONS COME FROM?

Where *do* emotions come from anyway? I hear people say things like, "Depression runs in my family." So are emotions simply genetics? Yet we all know emotions happen when life events happen. For example, I feel crappy when I hear about yet another act of violence in the world, and I feel exhilarated when I'm alone with a jar of peanut butter and a spoon. So it can't be *just* genetics that creates emotion, can it? But sometimes *thinking* alone causes an emotion to swing one way or another—I feel a moment of peace when I think about sitting on my porch in the summer. I feel crappy when I think about paying the bills. So what the heck is going on here? Are emotions physical? Situational? Cognitive? When we really stop and think about it, emotions are slippery and wily creatures that seem to come at us from nowhere and everywhere.

To boot, our emotions are constantly shifting and changing, and we feel more than one emotion at the same time. We might be giddy to be doing something fun but equally worried about what's not getting attended to while we're having fun. We might find parenting to be both misery inducing and our greatest joy. We might deeply love our partners and at the same time wonder what the buckwheat pancake we were thinking when we chose them. We might take pride in our jobs, but equally find them tedious. We might love being alive and simultaneously find life unfulfilling. It can be confusing to diagnose someone with anxiety or depression when emotions are a constantly moving target.

One explanation for why we experience so many emotions is because *emotions are coming from different places at the same time.* And what's happening in one area of emotion may contradict what's happening in another. The science of emotion is still in its early stages, and the field of psychology has conflicting views about where emotions come from. So keep in mind that you will read different theories of emotions in other books. However, in a mind-body-spirit approach to emotions, I believe that all human emotions come from four primary sources. These four sources are as follows:

SOURCE #1: OUR CIRCUMSTANCES

That emotions come from our circumstances is a big fat "duh." Show me someone whose favorite sports team just won, or who was recently proposed to, or who just shared a terrific meal with friends, or whose children are quietly napping, and I'll show you someone with a positive emotion. Show me someone whose house was just destroyed by a hurricane, or whose car won't start, or who just got laid off from their job, or whose children do not want said nap, and I'll show you someone with crappy emotions.

To boot, our *past* circumstances can also play a significant role in how we feel currently, and this is particularly true for those who have experienced trauma or poverty or abuse. Additionally, the circumstances of the world, such as hearing about violence or environmental decline or the suffering of others can also deeply influence our emotional state.

What's happening or has happened in our external world impacts our mood. When we like what's happening or has happened in our lives or on the planet we feel good. When we don't like what's happening or has happened in our lives or on the planet we feel crappy. It doesn't take a fancy-schmancy book to tell you that.

One way to improve our emotions
is to improve our circumstances.
But you already knew that one …

This is where we tend to focus our attention when it comes to changing our emotions. We try, as much as we're able, to alter the circumstances that are driving the crappy emotions. We apply for a new job or look for a new boyfriend or buy new sparkly things or start a new health regimen or move to a new neighborhood or vote for a new president or... Unfortunately, changing our circumstances to change our moods is not a sustainable formula for emotional well-being. Most things happening in our lives and on our planet simply can't be changed, at least not overnight, and often not by our single-handed efforts alone. Even if we were able to obtain our ideal circumstances, life is an ever-changing quagmire of experience, so those perfect circumstances will be temporary at best.

Now I'm not saying never change your circumstances. In situations when you can change your mood by changing something external in your life, by all means change your circumstances. If working toward a new position or a new career lifts you, *do it*. If ending a stale relationship makes you feel hopeful inside, *free yourself* and your partner. If fighting for a cause you believe in gives you a reason to get out of bed in the morning, *fight*. And for the love of all things you can melt cheese on, if your circumstances contain any form of violence, please, please, *please* do all you can to change your circumstances.

However, when altering your circumstances is just not possible, I promise that we have other options for shifting our emotional state. When life is bigger than our ability to change it, we must turn to the other three sources of emotion to lift our mood. Read on to learn where we can truly pack a wallop when it comes to generating positive feelings and getting rid of crappy ones.

SOURCE #2: THE BODY

Our body is the physical vessel through which we navigate our circumstances. When the body is rested, nourished and gently exercised, we feel positive emotions. When the body is imbalanced—for example when we are fatigued, malnourished, ill, or unfit—we feel some form of crappy. Show me someone, for example, who drinks caffeinated beverages all day, and I will show you someone prone to anxiety and irritability. Show me someone with insomnia, and I will show you someone who feels depressed and foggy. Show me someone who has just eaten a hot meal loaded with good fats, and I will show you someone who feels she can take on the world.

We don't really consider the sensations of our body "emotions." We can say our bodies feel tired or sick, but we don't say, "My body feels sad," or "My body feels irritable." That said, when a body is balanced and healthy, it feeds into our good moods, and when a body is out of balance or unhealthy, it lays the foundation for a crappy mood.

As an aside, if you see a psychiatrist or a medical doctor for your bad mood, you will often be treated with an antidepressant or related medication. And, while this might be beneficial if the source of your emotion is physical, if your negative emotion is coming from one of the other three sources of emotions, the use of medication as an intervention certainly becomes debatable.

Additionally, antidepressants target neurotransmitters in the brain, and while this is one possible source of physical imbalance that can lead to crappy emotions, there are arguably many other imbalances that could be the root cause of crappy emotions that antidepressants don't address. For example, depression, anxiety, and irritability could be a sign of a lack of certain nutrients, or underlying illness, or dehydration, or a poorly functioning digestive system, or poor sleep, or too much processed food, or …

One way to improve our emotions is to deeply tune into
and meet the needs of the body.

Positive emotions increase when we tune into the cues and messages of our bodies. Our bodies communicate with us all day long, telling us "Yes, no, maybe … " The body has energy when it wants to do something, or it feels tired when it needs sleep. It is hungry when it craves nourishment, or it is sated when it's time to rest and digest. It tenses when it doesn't like something, and it relaxes when it's happy. It becomes uncomfortable in the wrong temperature, and comfortable when we dress it just right. When it senses we are in danger, it sends out all sorts of warning signals, such as a racing heart and a flush of heat. And sometimes it takes over completely (we call this our reflexes) and steers us toward safety.

For some reason, we have learned that the communications from the body should not be taken too seriously. Instead, we tend to ignore, or even shun, signals of fatigue or tension or discomfort. We treat the body like a petulant child who needs to be disciplined and controlled. If the body is hungry, we say it shouldn't be hungry or it will get fat. If it's tired, we tell it to "buck up," we have work to do. When it tenses against a decision we're making, we ignore it and drag ourselves forward anyway. When it's full and doesn't want anything more to eat, we pretend not to notice as we lick our plates clean. When it needs a break from the computer, we tell it there's no time.

In fact, many of us have done such a stellar job of ignoring and denying the body, we can't even hear its signals anymore. To boot, we have a plethora of readily available substances that override and confuse the natural signals of the body. Addictive substances such as sugar, caffeine, alcohol, processed foods, and nicotine saturate the body with *cravings* rather than cues, and these cravings smother the body's deeper abilities to make its needs known to us.

Why are we so insistent on tuning out our bodily cues of tension and ease? Because we have learned, I'm not sure when or where, not to trust the body. We fear that letting the body have its way would land us on the couch, smearing cookie dough and potato chips all over ourselves, taking ridiculously satisfying naps and foregoing every professional, social, or domestic obligation of our day. We see the body as something to conquer, discipline, manage, and deprive. We believe that it is mind *over* body, not mind-body.

But the belief that our bodies can't be trusted is a false one. Honestly, it's just plain malarkey. If we were to *truly listen* to the needs of our bodies, over time we would see that there is a natural balance in its signals to us. Sometimes the body has energy. Sometimes it craves restoration. Sometimes the body wants comfort food. Sometimes it's not really all that hungry. Sometimes the body wants to be social and active. Sometimes the body warns us that certain people require more caution or distance. When the body is nourished and rested, it gives us natural energy to navigate our outer world tasks. When it isn't cared for and doesn't agree with the daily schedule, or certain relationships, or a particular choice, it tenses.

And when this tension and lack of care are habitual and chronic, we become prone to injury or illness or, even worse, disease, all of which force us to *finally* listen to the needs and signals of the body and take them more seriously.

I can hear your mind spinning and saying, "But Heidi, there is absolutely no way I can attend to my hectic days while also honoring the needs of my body. It's just a reality that in order to keep up with all of life's obligations and duties, the body needs to toughen up and gut through."

I hear and understand your concern, I truly do. It's true that there are times we have to dismiss the information provided by the body in favor of reality. But all of us, and I mean every single human on this planet, could do a better job of listening to our bodies more actively and more often. And all of us, every single one of us, could do a better job of incorporating the messages the body sends us into our daily decisions and behaviors, our lifestyle choices, our food choices, our choices in relationships, and our calendaring choices. If we did this even a little bit, the body would thank us with positive feelings.

SOURCE #3: THE SPIRIT

The spirit can be described in many ways: our highest selves, our values, the part of us that produces wisdom and allows us to feel purpose. If you're religious, you may call a spirit a soul. If you're new-agey, you might say your spirit houses your intuition and connects you to the universe. If you're an atheist, you might call a spirit your best self. If you're a neurologist, you might say the spirit is your prefrontal cortex. If you're a teenager, you might call your spirit your heart. If you're a stoner, you might just say, "Whoaaaa, dude."

At the end of the day, no matter what you call it, "spirit" is our ability to feel alive. It is our ability to experience life as more than the sum of its parts. We all know what it feels like to be tuned into our highest selves, at least for short durations of time. During these moments, we sense that our lives have a purpose or meaning. We experience compassion for ourselves and others. We care for the greater world. We are aware of our values. Whenever we feel fulfilled or connected or inspired or wise or creative or purposeful, we are living in a place of spirit.

For most of us, a deeper connection to spirit happens in what appears to be a random or willy-nilly way. We don't stop and think about why or how our higher selves have kicked into gear. And we don't really learn how to directly access our higher selves, let alone live from this place. Sure, many people go to their religious institutions for a place to tune into their spirit. Others find nature or meditation. But these tend to be compartmentalized experiences. At the end of the day, spirit is experienced as a precious positive moment in our day (or maybe even week, month, or year) rather than utilized as a moment-to-moment guiding force.

When we engage in behaviors that align with our spirit, we feel positive emotions. When we ignore or engage in behaviors that do not align with our deeper nature, we feel crappy. When we live a life that wakes up our spirit, we feel positive. When we live a life that numbs or dulls our spirit, we feel crappy.

Unfortunately, our culture has very specific rules about how a person *should* live regardless of how their spirit is wired. In American culture, we specifically espouse middle-class values encouraging all kids to go to college, get a job, buy a house, have a family with an opposite-sex partner, save for retirement, etc. While this trajectory might align with some spirits, many spirits are likely wired for completely different journeys and will experience an underlying sense of "crappy" no matter what's happening with the other three sources of emotion.

One way to improve emotions is to cultivate a life
that expands the spirit.

Spirit speaks to us all day long, but we tend to tune out its feedback. Everyone has a different relationship with spirit, but for most of us, we feel some sort of deep internal constriction or expansion, or lightness or heaviness, in a way that's hard to explain. The awareness of spirit is not an acute physical sensation like it is in the body. When our spirit feels full and at peace, we experience a sense of openness or lightening in the center of our bodies. And when life feels out of alignment with our values or nature, our spirit dims or contracts.

Think of how you feel when you are on vacation and see the perfect sunset. Something inside of you softens. Now think of how you feel when you contemplate a future without a new episode of *Game of Thrones* ever again. Something inside of you goes into the fetal position. The spirit "tightens" or becomes "heavy" when it is saying no and "softens" or "expands" or "brightens" or "lightens" when it is saying yes, and it is doing this all day every day.

Just as with the communications of the body, we don't trust listening to our spirit because we fear we will become irresponsible and self-indulgent. We fear that if we only follow what makes our spirit expand, we will quit our jobs, let our children run around like savages, listen to music and dance all the livelong day, lose all drive and ambition, and forgo all sensibility and discipline. (Is it just me, or does that sound heavenly to anyone else?)

However, just like we can trust our bodies more than we realize, we can also tune into and trust our spirits. After all, your spirit is wise and value driven. It wants to guide you toward a life of purpose, passion, meaning and connection. It wants you to make decisions that align with your deepest nature and the nature of the greater good.

SOURCE #4: THE MIND

The mind is the part of ourselves that is chattering all day long. It tells us what we need to get done in a day. It tells us how to solve problems. It tells us how to navigate the tasks and events of our days. "Get in the left lane." "Go to the bank before the grocery store." "Set up a training schedule for that 5k." "Tell your teen to pick up his socks." "Get that email done before the next meeting." That's what the mind is good for.

The mind also keeps track of the standards and rules it thinks we should live by. As a result, the voice of the mind can be very judging. Oh boy, can it be judging. "You should do this." "You shouldn't do that." "He should do this." "She shouldn't do that." "It was bad that you did this." "It was good that you did that."

The mind is the commander and chief of the outer world, and it thrives on managing, managing, managing, and judging, judging, judging. It thrives on setting goals and accomplishing them, and if you don't accomplish them, it equally thrives on telling you what you did wrong and why you are a failure. All day long, the mind is telling us, "You need to. You have to. You've got to. You should. They need to. They have to. They've got to. They should." It's like the Little Engine That Could on bad diesel. Conversely, the mind likes to hold underlying judgments, and it's usually something like this: "You're not *doing* enough. You don't *have* enough. You are *not* enough."

So if the spirit feels exhilarating emotions when it is living its nature, and the body feels positive when it is safe, nourished and rested, what makes the mind feel good? Lots of things, actually: solving problems, living up to standards and expectations, meeting goals and objectives, being logical. But the mind primarily thrives on impressing and accomplishing. Oh, how the mind loves accomplishments, big and small. It loves when it accomplishes its to-do list, and it loves when it does something notable that can be insta'd on Instagram or chirped about on Twitter. The mind thrives on achieving and gaining approval. And when we aren't achieving or aren't being impressive, the mind equally thrives on berating us and telling us we are not doing or being enough.

The mind, alongside body and spirit, is a very important instrument on our human dashboard—especially when the mind is used effectively to help us navigate the basic events of our day. But the mind only responds to rules, goals, objectives, and standards. When something follows one of the mind's rules or achieves one of the mind's standards, or accomplishes one of the mind's objectives, a brief positive emotion is experienced. When a rule, goal, or expectation is not met, the mind jumps into code red. The mind is happy when its "shoulds" are met. The mind is negative and judging when they're not.

THE PROBLEM WITH THE MIND ...

One (not so effective) way to improve emotions is to meet ALL of the expectations, standards, rules and goals of the mind.

Check off every item on your to-do list, work out five days a week, earn an impressive salary, take on impressive goals and meet them in a disciplined and methodical way, be charming in every social situation, use the latest theory of parenting, furnish the perfect house and keep it perfectly clean, get whiter teeth, perfectly follow all your food rules, and ALWAYS have a perfect hair day. Be productive and achieve something valuable in every freakin' nanosecond of every freakin' day. Strive, accomplish, master, tackle, surmount, overcome, triumph, conquer, push, force, win. AT EVERYTHING. That will make the mind a little bit happy for a brief moment here and there.

Or ...

We can improve emotions by quieting the mind and bringing it into alignment with body and spirit.

When we triage the mind with the body and the spirit, these instruments can work together to help us make decisions, choose our behaviors and direct the course of our lives. The body communicates to us with tension and ease and provides us with energy. The mind helps us navigate outer-world challenges and feels good when its standards are appeased. The spirit informs us of inner-world needs and feels expansive when its nature and values are fulfilled.

However, there's a minor problem here, and that is a sarcastic way of saying there's a really big problem. The mind is the trickiest source of emotion to quell. Our standards and expectations for ourselves and others keep going up and up and up and up, and our belief of what can get accomplished or should get accomplished in a day is overwhelming.

I believe this to be a modern-day phenomenon—something our ancestors did not struggle with to the same extent. As a world, we have come to value the standards and expectations of the mind at the expense of the body and the spirit. The mind is even first on the list. Have you ever noticed we never say spirit-body-mind connection? Or body-mind connection?

As a world, we have really come to worship the power and value of the mind. We believe that a well-developed mind can conquer all. Where do we send our children as soon as they're old enough? To school, of course. We don't send them into the great outdoors to help them cultivate their strength, flexibility and physical health. We don't send them to a meditation center to contemplate their deeper spirits and life purpose. We send them to school to develop their minds. It is the mind in which we invest.

To boot, the 21ˢᵗ-century addition of a *virtual* reality has only compounded the problem of a mind-driven world. We now engage with almost everything—people, places, things—using our minds and not our bodies (or arguably our spirits). As we manage our emails and texts, update our Google calendars, navigate our phone apps, do our online shopping, complete our online trip planning, it is the mind that is active.

Meanwhile, our bodies are lucky to get dragged to the gym for 30 minutes so that our minds can smugly check off "work out" from our to-do list. And our spirits may get some gratuitous attention on holidays, weekends, or our once-a-year vacations. But it isn't long before the mind regains control and starts dictating what we need to, have to, got to and should do. Where the mind, body and spirit are ideally meant to be working in harmony, in reality the mind has become an oppressive dictator, with the body and spirit being its fearful minions. We are out of balance. We have forgotten how to listen to the wisdom of the body and spirit.

But here's the good news. We are starting to get it. If you are reading this book, it's because a part of you already knows everything I just said. Your body likely softens ever so slightly at the recognition that your mind has been trying to control it, and your spirit is expansively saying, "Read more please." Meanwhile, your mind begrudgingly writes "read book" on its to-do list, and tells you don't forget to take out the garbage, feed the dog, and don't let anyone see the title of this book because it's not very intellectual and impressive.

TYING IT ALL TOGETHER ...

Our emotional experiences are the collective results of our circumstantial, physical, mental and spiritual experiences.

This is a very important statement, so I'm going to emphatically say it again. Our emotional experiences are the *collective results* of our circumstantial, physical, mental and spiritual experiences. That is why our emotions can feel so topsy-turvy and conflicted. One thing can be happening in our circumstances, another in our bodies, yet another in our minds and another still in our spirits. Additionally, all four sources of emotions can influence one another, so if something is happening in one area, it can trigger a response in another.

Have you ever had circumstances where you thought you *should* feel happy and you don't? As an example, over the holiday season? Culture tells us that December is a time for gaiety, tradition, and celebration. But what are your circumstances, really? Is Uncle Albert bound to get drunk and slobbery, and is your sister going to harp on your mother *again* about the evils of her gluten-filled baked goods? And anyone want to place a wager on how many seconds it takes before your father-in-law begins yet another one of his endless political rants?

And circumstances are only one part of our emotions. What's happening with you physically during this time? Will you sleep and lovingly nourish your body, or will you be using every waking second defending your home against the destruction of children with cookie-induced mania? And what's happening in your mind? Has its standard of "clean the house, prep the gifts, have the perfect meal prepared, find the perfect outfit and look good in that perfect outfit, create well-behaved children, spend equal time with both sides of the family" been appeased? Or has the mind found a thousand standards and expectations that you and those around you will fail.

And your spirit? Is it even present? Have you taken a moment to truly consider what would make it expand? Or has the body been too numb and the mind been too tyrannical for you to even notice your poor spirit? Overall you might appreciate the idea of the holidays, but the moment-to-moment reality of this time, when we examine all four sources of emotions, may be a conflicted and contradictory experience.

Identifying the four sources of emotions sounds simple enough, doesn't it? But it can be challenging to tell exactly where an emotion is coming from, especially since the sources of emotions all overlap and affect one another. However, knowing the four sources of emotion supplies us with an immediate starting point for understanding our emotions. The four sources of emotion also give us a road map for shifting our emotional state.

As an example, when I wrote this, it was March in Minnesota. For my fellow Midwesterners, you know this is a miserably drab time of year. The snow that initially seemed magical now has the charm of your partner's morning breath. And rather than doing fun winter activities with your family, like sledding and building snowpeople, you plug them in front of their iPads and throw them crackers and hot dogs once a day. No matter how you slice it, March in Minnesota is a wash.

However, if one evaluates the four sources of emotion, one can more adroitly identify the changes that can be made to shift that dismal March mood. For example, here's my March protocol:

What's happening in my *circumstances*?

It's beat-your-forehead-against-a-wall GRAY outside and there isn't a gosh darn thing I can do about it. However, I can improve my circumstances ever so slightly by putting on the one remaining clean pair of yoga pants, picking up the living room a little bit, turning on some soft music, and researching new shows to binge-watch later that night. It doesn't bring the sun, but it helps a little bit.

What's happening in my *body*?

I do a brief scan and can luckily say I have been sleeping well. I did have wine the evening before so perhaps I can lift the energy of my body by hydrating (we'll talk about this in Chapter 5). And because it's been so sunless, I decide to take an extra dose of vitamin D3, as well as do some stimulating breath work (again, stay tuned). This does not change the unrelenting gray, but being proactive about my health in small ways does lift me a little bit.

Okay, the *mind* is next.

Oh, the tootin-fallutin' mind. My mind is going on and on (and on) about all the things I *should* be accomplishing—exercise, housecleaning, catching up on communications, running errands, prepping for the week. My mind believes these things should happen rain or shine or blizzard or apocalyptic zombie attack. Though I can't totally shut up my mind, I do firmly tell it that humans were likely meant to slow down during March. I reassure the mind that its standards and expectations will be attended to another day—likely in June. My mind does not like this one bit, but it's going to have to deal with it.

Finally, the *spirit*.

Ahh, the spirit. I look inward and ask myself, "What do I deeply crave?" And in March, my spirit craves coddling. It craves cancelling social commitments with others (which luckily—their spirits crave, too). It wants music and maybe a little journaling. So I coo and whisper to my deepest self that I will do my best to meets its needs. I will keep the day as slow as humanly possible and engage in quiet activities. I will talk to myself and others in a loving way. I will allow life to be easy in March.

There—I've attended to all four sources of emotion. My living room is picked up, my body is hydrated and filled with extra vitamin D. My mind has been shushed. My spirit is being honored. Has my "blah" mood morphed into euphoria? Not quite, but admittedly I'm close. Understanding the four sources of emotion makes an emotion less overwhelming. To boot, it can be quite enjoyable to consider and influence the four sources of emotions to the best of our abilities.

CHAPTER SUMMARY

Emotions are more complicated than "I feel happy" or "I feel sad." This is because our emotions are born from four different sources.

Our circumstances are the first source of emotion. When good things happen in our lives, we feel good. When bad things happen in our lives, we feel crappy.

Emotions come from our body as well. When the body is rested and nourished and has been given the proper amount of movement, we feel positive emotions. When the body is tired, doped up on sugar or caffeine, or has an underlying imbalance, we feel negative emotions.

The mind is the third source of emotion. When the mind accomplishes something on its "need to, have to, got to, should" list, a positive emotion is generated. When a standard or expectation of the mind is not met, we experience a negative emotion. As an added note, not meeting the standards and expectations of the mind is arguably *the primary contributor* toward many people's modern-day negative emotions.

Finally, emotions come from our spirit. When the spirit experiences the beauty of nature, the warmth of genuine human connection, or the thrill of creative expression, a positive feeling is generated. When the spirit is ignored, or engaged in activities that don't align with its values, or deprived of experiences that ignite or vitalize, it feels crappy. Emotions are the collective result of our circumstantial, physical, mental, and spiritual experiences.

But Heidi, why in the world do we have so many crappy emotions? Well, that's for the next chapter ...

CHAPTER 3

WHY IN THE WORLD DO WE HAVE SO MANY CRAPPY EMOTIONS?

We've already established that emotions are besieging us from all angles, and naming our exact emotional state is tricky when we really look at it. Not only are emotions derived from the four sources of circumstances, body, mind and spirit, but they change (sometimes strongly, most of the time subtly) throughout the days, hours, minutes, seconds. Moment to moment, we fluctuate from irked to worried to pleased to fed up to contented to excited to neutral to dread-filled to relieved, etc. Strung together, our emotions are a lively and entertaining melody.

It is important to note that these fluctuating emotions are not a defect. They are not random experiences that simply need to be tolerated. *Emotions have a purpose.* Positive emotions tell us something is in balance, either in our circumstances, our bodies, our minds, or our spirits. Crappy emotions alert us to imbalance in at least one of these same four areas. Our job is to see if we can identify the source of imbalance and tend to it.

To help us better understand the logic of emotions, it might be helpful to start with an evolutionary examination of emotions. Why would we, as living creatures, be given these strange inner experiences to begin with? Sensations like hunger and fatigue and sex drive are easy to understand. To endure as a species, we needed those feelings to help us meet our basic needs for survival. But what about emotions? Do they have any actual purpose in the human experience other than telling us whether something is pleasurable or not?

Yes. At least theoretically.

Let's take a look at the following diagram as one way to loosely, but conveniently, organize our negative emotional experiences.

STRESS
Circumstantial, Physical, Mental and Spiritual

Fight	Flight	Freeze
annoyed, cranky, ticked, irritated, resentful, belligerent, frustrated, angry, mad, indignant, upset, fuming, furious, enraged	***(includes a high-arousal freeze response)*** *worried, apprehensive, concerned, nervous, distressed, frightened, shocked, on edge, anxious, phobic, paranoid, panicked*	***(our "play dead" response)*** *melancholy, low, "blah," crummy, numb, mournful, sad, blue, glum, in the dumps, crestfallen, despondent, mournful, depressed*

We're all intimately familiar with the word "stress," and if you're like me, even hearing the word invokes it. Generally stress makes us think of the aspects of our lives that generate stress, such as our jobs, our schedule, our homes, our finances, other people, etc. But in addition to being created by our circumstances, stress can also be produced by the body, the mind, and the spirit. When we don't sleep or tend to our health, what do we feel? Stress. When our mind becomes fixated on a certain expectation or goal, what do we feel? S-t-r-e-double-s. And when our spirits are thinking that we're not on the right life path for us, we feel stressed, stressed, stressed.

As humans, when we feel stress, we tend to have one of three knee-jerk stress responses. We either fight stress, or we flee from stress, or we freeze in the face of stress. Each stress response can be paired with a spectrum of emotions. When you experience anything from mild annoyance to fiery rage, you are experiencing a form of "fight." When you experience anything from niggling worry to pure panic, you are in your "flight" mode. And when you experience anything ranging between "blah" to woefully depressed, you are in "freeze" mode.

It is perhaps important to note that, although science has not explored this to date that I know of, I believe there are actually *two* versions of the human freeze mode. There is a high-arousal freeze state where our bodies seize, our hearts race, and our thoughts spin. Think of hearing a loud noise late at night. What do you initially do? Seize up and panic! This type of freezing is, loosely stated, a *flight* response where the gas pedal is down, but the car won't go. The emotions generated from this state are the exact same emotions generated in a flight state—anx-anx-anxious. When you're experiencing a lot of "spinning wheels," but find you're helpless to take action, you are in this mode.

Then there is a low-arousal freeze state that, to date, is little studied or understood. In this state, our brain hits the brakes on our sympathetic nervous system and sends our body into a slump where we lack energy, lose motivation, become numb to the world, and feel some shade of a low mood. This mode may more aptly be called our "play dead" response, but to stay consistent with the current literature, this is what is being referred to as a freeze response throughout this book.

Confused? Let's summarize it this way. If you run into a bear in the woods, you have four options. You can 1) Fight for your life. That's our fight response. You can 2) RUN! 3) Or you can *want* to run, but your body stays paralyzed. Both of those I am calling our flight response. Finally, you can 4) Go limp and play dead. This is our freeze response.

A MODERN-DAY TWIST ON STRESS

Hypothetically, it's not hard to see how the primary stress responses of fight, flight, or freeze would have been useful back in more primitive times. When someone was invading your territory, you should probably fight for your life! And when an animal was charging after you, you'd better run for your life! And if you heard something in the woods that could be dangerous, high-arousal freezing sounds like a smart response to me. And when we experienced something that required healing, like illness or grief or overexertion, a freeze or "play dead" response forced our poor bodies to disengage from the world. Fight, flight, and freeze responses made perfect sense for the original stressors dealt with by humans.

Alas, in the modern world, we still have stressors and we still respond to these stressors with variations of fight, flight, and freeze, but the formula has become much more complicated. First, while our more primitive life stressors could be life-threatening, our current-day stressors, for many of us at least, are usually more arbitrary in nature. We aren't stressed about our homes being invaded, we're stressed about whether our house is picked up and impressively decorated.

And many of us are lucky enough not to be stressed about how we're going to get our next meal, but instead, we're stressed about what food choices to make and how we look in the clothes we're wearing. And today, most of us aren't too concerned about dangerous natural predators, but we are stressed about what our colleagues, friends and family think about us. To boot, in the 21st century we aren't stressed for short durations of time while an acute danger is present. Instead, we are often chronically and habitually stressed, with little reprieve, in both abstract and concrete ways, all day, every day, over and over again.

And if chronic stress isn't stressful enough, the nature of our fight, flight and freeze responses have become more subtle and internalized, making them challenging to identify as stress responses. Instead of all-out fighting, we might inwardly become irritated with a colleague who is slow to do his part. Or instead of all-out running, we may harbor a constant undercurrent of fear for the future. Or instead of outwardly freezing, we might gut through our days with a smile on our face while feeling exhausted and lost on the inside.

Even though most of us reading this book are fortunate enough not to be experiencing life-threatening stressors, as a species we are collectively managing more stress than ever before, and it's occurring in pervasive and unrelenting ways. Without even realizing it, we are actively using our fight, flight, and freeze responses throughout our days, all day, every day.

In a nutshell, life is full of stressors. These stressors come in the form of circumstantial stressors, physical stressors, mental stressors, and spiritual stressors. When we experience stress, our instinctive reaction is a fight, flight, or freeze response, and each stress response is accompanied by its own spectrum of emotions. When we are in fight mode, we can experience anything from annoyance to rage. When we are in flight mode (or high-arousal freeze mode), we experience anything from worry to panic. And when we are in freeze mode, we experience some form of the blues.

It is important to note that we all experience all three stress responses. But when we look closely, most of us will find that we tend toward one of the stress responses more than the others. For example, my primary stress response seems to be fight, with a flight response coming in a close second. My freeze response is the least utilized of the three. My significant other, Pete, tends more toward a high-arousal freeze response. His fight response doesn't get used all that often. When we disagree on something, I roll my eyes, gesticulate spastically, and stomp my feet like they're on fire. Pete, on the other hand, stays stone still, even though he wants to run, until I get all of the sizzle out of me. All of us are wired a smidge differently.

P.S. Some emotions, like shame or grief, are a complex *combination* of our fight, flight, and freeze responses. Our stress-response system is capable of generating more than one stress response at the same time, and it's pretty impressive when you really stop and think about it.

THE PURPOSE OF EACH OF THE STRESS RESPONSES

The emotions connected with each stress response, albeit uncomfortable when directly experienced, theoretically have a purpose. For example, even though it isn't generally all that effective in the modern world, all forms of worry are trying to help us find escape routes for our problems.

> *Worry and anxiety are trying to give you the energy to get*
> *the heck away from a situation or out of a problem.*

And for many, your flight response is so constantly or intensely activated that you qualify for a diagnosis of generalized anxiety disorder—which is simply the label the modern psychological world puts on an overactive flight response. (P.S. If you have been diagnosed with generalized anxiety disorder, rest assured that you are not a freak of nature. While all of us are capable of all three stress responses—fight, flight and freeze—we all tend to favor one in particular. Your anxiety is simply indicative of a flight response that is chronically activated and working too hard. As an anxious person, you are constantly trying to flee from stress in your circumstances, your body, your mind, and your spirit, and that just happens to be your hardwired stress response. But believe you me, we all have responses to stress that spiral out of control, so please don't feel alone.)

Okay, what about sadness or melancholy? Why in the world have we humans developed the ability to feel such low moods? For our ancestors, it's not hard to see that low moods forced us to stay in bed when we needed some form of healing or rest.

> *Low moods carve out a way for us to disconnect from the world so*
> *that something can be tended to or healed internally.*

When we're blue or down, our bodies and minds slow down and become foggy. We don't feel like seeing anyone or doing anything. We close our curtains and pull the sheet over our heads. Having a sad day here or a "blah" week there forces us to take a break from our outer life so that we may cultivate our inner world or heal ourselves in some way. It's a perfectly healthy phenomenon in doses.

However, our culture does not generally allow people to listen to and honor their freeze response, nor do we teach people how to truly heal physically and emotionally when they're feeling low. Instead, we focus on how to "snap out of it and get back to business," which I believe only deepens the freeze response and makes it worse.

Just like anxiety, low moods have spiraled out of control for some due to circumstantial, physical, mental, or spiritual stressors. When someone's freeze response becomes overwhelming, they may be diagnosed with major depressive disorder. (P.S. If you have been diagnosed with major depressive disorder, rest assured that you are not a freak of nature either. Your depression is indicative of an overly strong freeze response. As a depressed person, your freeze response is trying to get you to disconnect from the outer world, and your job is to figure out why. Do you need a break from your circumstances? Or does your body need some sort of healing or balancing? Or is depression trying to numb the constant "need to, have to, got to, shoulds" of your mind? Or is a low mood trying to get you to look inward and study the needs of your deeper spirit?)

How about the purpose of anger? From an evolutionary perspective, it is not hard to see that emotions on the spectrum of anger—ranging from irritation to rage—are manifestations of our fight response.

Anger has the very important purpose of summoning strength.

Anger empowers us to protect ourselves from threats. However, just like a chronic or overly strong flight response becomes anxiety, and a chronic or overly strong freeze response becomes depression, a chronic or overly strong fight response becomes problematic when we are habitually angry about threats that aren't really threats.

Think about the last time you got angry. Was it because your food supply, your survival, your children, or your territory were in danger?

Most likely no. If you're like me, you were angry because your (now ex) boyfriend would leave his dishes anywhere and everywhere except the dishwasher, or your (now ex) boss would pile more on to your to-do list than a human could possibly do in a day, or your (now back in good standing) friend cancelled at the last minute—again. I'm not saying these phenomena shouldn't elicit a response, but we now become angry when our personal standards aren't met, not when an actual threat to our life occurs. However, if you are experiencing a real threat, not a perceived one, please become angry!

Even though anger is our system's way of protecting us and empowering us, it can be challenging to figure out what to do with anger when the threat that provoked it is an arbitrary one. The techniques explored in this book should help with that. For now, simply note that anger has a valuable purpose, and that purpose is to galvanize us to fight for something.

P.S. We don't have a clinical diagnosis for someone who is chronically ticked off or angry—in part because this is a challenging topic to study, measure and make scientific. Sometimes we might associate anger with a bipolar disorder or a rarely used "intermittent explosive disorder." Or we might pair anger with anxiety or depression and loosely call it "agitated anxiety" or "irritable depression."

The reality is, chronic anger is the hyper-manifestation of our fight response to life. If you are angrier than the average person, don't fret. Of the fight, flight, or freeze stress responses, you just have a stronger fight response. Over time, your unique challenge is to learn when the world benefits from your anger (perhaps fighting for a social cause or higher purpose) and when you need to find something else to do with it.

CAN WE TALK ABOUT A NICE EMOTION FOR A MOMENT?

Let's get to our favorite emotion: happiness. Why in the world would we be wired to feel good? What reason, from an evolutionary perspective, would we benefit from experiencing joy or excitement or peace? We can understand that negative emotions were designed to keep us safe, healthy and empowered. But is there any good cause for feeling positive emotions?

The theory goes, and it is theory only but I like it, that happiness teaches us about our nature. For example, when a cat is curled up in a ray of sun, it is living its nature and is happy. When it is dressed in a onesie and put into a baby stroller, it is not living its nature and is definitively *not* happy and will claw at the human who did this (has anyone else learned this the hard way?). When we humans are happy, something is going right in either our circumstances, the body, the spirit, or the mind.

For example, we feel amazing after a good night's sleep (that is the body telling us "good job"), we have a rush of pride after a goal is achieved (the mind is happy when something is accomplished), and we feel a burst of vitality in our spirits when we see something beautiful like a news clip of a dog ecstatic to see his owner after a long military deployment (sob!). Happiness teaches us who we are, what makes us tick, where we should put our energy, and how we should live our best lives. Happiness helps us understand our truest and best selves at the levels of body, mind, and spirit. Except there is a catch …

Our modern-day minds have obtained a foothold on our happiness, and this happiness is often at the expense of our bodies and spirits.

The mind tends to feel happy when a problem is solved, or a goal is accomplished, or an expectation is met, or approval is received, or an inner "rule" of some sort has been followed. We feel a jolt of positive emotion when we've successfully completed our to-do list, or impressed our coworkers, or received a lot of "likes" on Facebook, and we put a lot of energy into these sorts of endeavors.

But if we truly take a moment to examine this mind-driven form of happiness, we will see it is short-lived and does not run very deep. Mind happiness is a glimmer of "Look at me, yippee!" but this rush is quickly replaced by the next to-do list item to be conquered, the next standard to be upheld, the next accomplishment to impress with.

Meanwhile, happiness derived at the level of spirit provides a deeper sense of well-being. When we are outdoors in natural beauty, or when we use our creativity, or when we live our deepest values, or when we are feeling close to others, we feel a sense of happiness in our hearts more than in our heads. When we make decisions that align with our innermost natures, such as participating in meaningful work, or taking steps to fulfill a lifelong dream, or engaging in behaviors that reflect our core values, something deep within us expands.

At times, this expansion might contradict what the mind wants or says is appropriate, but spirit happiness is a deeply satisfying and enduring feeling. Let's go back to my description of March in Minnesota as an example. On a gray, drab day, my mind wanted to be productive and get its to-do list done. That would have made my mind happy. In fact, productivity is the only thing that ever makes the boring mind happy. My spirit, on the other hand, wanted a soulful period of taking it easy and being reflective. The spirit, however, has more diversity when it comes to happiness. In March, it wanted a slow pace, but in June, it often craves vitality and activity.

In a perfect world, we would have two different words for mind-happy and spirit-happy, and maybe we do. Spirit-happiness might better be called "well-being," and mind-happiness could easily be reframed as "pride." Though we all need prideful moments every once in a while, most of us are hungry for a form of happiness that is more substantive than, "Look at me! Look at what obligations I just fulfilled and what tasks I just accomplished! Look at how impressive I am!" That's what this book is about—cultivating happiness not just in the mind, but also in the body and the spirit. This book is about softening pride and fostering well-being.

THE CURRENT MEDICAL MODEL OF EMOTIONS

To warn you, the view of emotions I've just outlined differs from how some conventionally trained psychologists might view negative emotions. In the current system of psychology, we do not generally view negative emotions as stress responses that have a purpose, nor do we deeply explore the sources of stress from a circumstances-mind-body-spirit perspective.

Instead, we have a diagnostic system for organizing persistent negative emotions as "disorders," much in the same way the medical world organizes physical health symptoms as diseases. We outline these mental health disorders in a large and tedious book called the *DSM-5*™, where we look primarily at the physical symptoms of negative emotions, such as lack of concentration, sleep changes, appetite changes, and behavioral changes.

The problem with this system is that these "diagnoses," while they effectively label a collection of mental health symptoms, do not give us information about the *causes* of those symptoms. And because psychological diagnoses are organized much like medical diagnoses, there is an unspoken assumption, even if we don't directly say it, that they need to be treated like medical issues—with medications.

Calling depression or anxiety a "disorder," in my view of emotions, is like calling a cough a disease. A cough is a symptom, not a disease. And it can be a symptom of a scratchy throat, a simple virus, a deeper infection, asthma or allergies, or a more serious concern like cancer.

But in the end, a cough is a symptom, not a diagnosis. I believe the same is true for most of our negative emotions. Depression and anxiety and anger are symptoms of imbalance, and imbalance can occur in our circumstances, our bodies, our minds, and our spirits.

Another confusing component of labeling strong negative experiences as "disorders" is that it makes it seem like something atypical or pathological is taking place, when that is often not the case. For example, when someone is experiencing the low mood and hopelessness associated with the death of a loved one, this is called major depressive *disorder*. But many believe it seems much more reasonable (not to mention humane) to call this a normal depressive *response*.

When someone is navigating a challenging time, such as a divorce or a job transition, we call it an adjustment *disorder*—but isn't this just a predictable adjustment *response*? Or when someone is having a hard time managing the stress of a traumatic experience, we call it post-traumatic stress *disorder,* making it shameful, when really it is a deeply understandable post-traumatic stress *response.*

Diagnosing emotions makes us very confused about what is and isn't a normal emotional experience, and diagnosing emotions makes it seem like we need to medically treat the people experiencing those emotions. Diagnoses also isolate individuals, making them feel that there is something biologically wrong with them.

What if we were to call strong emotions "responses" rather than "disorders"? And once it is ascertained whether someone is experiencing a fight response, a flight response, or a freeze response (or a combination thereof), the next step is to figure out the source of the stress. Tough circumstances? Imbalance in the body? Rigid rules in the mind? An ignored spirit? All of the above?

Now, to be fair, some mental health issues are solely medical disorders. Schizophrenia or bipolar disorder are good examples (although I personally believe many people are misdiagnosed with bipolar disorder when, in reality, they are just experiencing very strong stress responses). This book does not address mental health problems of a purely clinical nature. But for our three key stress responses of anger, anxiety, or depression, we, in my opinion, waste a lot of time trying to distinguish between normal and "disordered." And we treat strong negative emotions as "illness," when they may be better approached as symptoms of imbalance in either our circumstances, body, mind, or spirit.

Explaining and categorizing emotions is a murky and complex subject with much area for discussion, but at the end of the day, I think many of us agree (professionals and nonprofessionals alike) that the current diagnostic system creates more questions than answers and more confusion than therapeutic direction. Said again, in a mind-body-spirit approach to emotions, anger, anxiety and depression are fight, flight and freeze responses, not medical diagnoses. And these stress responses show us that something needs to be attended to in our circumstances, our health, our minds, or our spirits.

So how do I assess clients from this more holistic perspective? First of all, I examine the four levels of stress in their lives. What are their *circumstantial* stressors—both current challenges being dealt with and past ones that haven't healed? Do they have draining jobs? A strained relationship? Past abuse or trauma? Money struggles? Are they being discriminated against? What stressors are impacting them *physically*? Are they not sleeping? Do they eat a lot of junk food or drink a lot of alcohol? Do they have any physical illnesses? What stressors are products of their *mind* and the way they are thinking? Are they perfectionistic? Are they overly concerned about what others think? Do they have rigid standards that they or others aren't living up to? Is their life driven by a to-do list? What stressors are coming from a place of *spirit*? Are they struggling to figure out what makes them tick? Do they feel angst for the world and humankind? Are they living a life that goes against their core values?

After assessing the various life stressors, I gauge whether clients are coping with these stressors using a fight, flight, or freeze response—or a combination thereof. I also loosely hypothesize the possible *purpose* of their particular stress response. Is someone chronically irritable because he is trying to get the power to change his circumstances? Is his body irritated as a way to signal a food sensitivity or a need for more restful sleep? Is someone anxious because she is physically sensitive to caffeine and sugar? Is anxiety trying to give her mind the energy to seek solutions to problems? Is depression trying to numb a mind that is constantly telling them they're not good enough? Is depression their body's freeze response to a lack of key nutrients?

When all of this information is in place, I have a comprehensive therapeutic framework that helps me see where my client and I need to focus our efforts. Here are a few examples:

CHRONICALLY DEPRESSED FOR OVER A DECADE

Leo has been chronically depressed for over a decade. He had been formally diagnosed with major depressive disorder and had tried many medications, as well as electric convulsive therapy, but nothing provided relief. Leo's sleep is poor and his diet is abysmal. Leo eats primarily fast-food and drinks soda several times a day. He is prediabetic. Leo says he has been mildly depressed for as long as he can remember, but his depression worsened when his wife left him for another man.

Around this same time, he was let go from his job for underperforming. Leo hated that job, since it was a desk job, and he craved motion and being outdoors. He had always wanted to work for the National Park Service but studied technology because the pay was better and there were more job opportunities. Leo was eventually granted disability for his depression, but finances have been an ongoing stressor. Leo plays video games with a friend every once in a while, but other than that, does little socially. Leo feels lethargic and depressed most of the time. He feels he has little reason to live.

Leo has several circumstantial stressors—finances are difficult for him and he is isolated socially. He has the past stressors of a broken marriage and being fired from his job. Physically, Leo's body is stressed from lack of sleep, little exercise and poor diet. Mentally, Leo experiences a high level of negative self-talk and an ongoing sense of failing internal goals, standards, and expectations. Spiritually, Leo has little that gives him purpose or meaning, and he chose a career path that did not align with his true nature. Leo's primary stress response is to freeze. Physically, he freezes by feeling sluggish and slow. Mentally, his mind is foggy and he has a hard time making decisions. Spiritually, he describes himself as numb and feels disconnected from a sense of purpose or meaning.

Although I can only theorize, I believe depression is trying to get Leo to slow down, look inward, and create a life more in line with his spirit. Additionally, because of his poor physical health, depression might be his body's way of slowing down so he can heal and recover—although Leo will need to aid that recovery with better lifestyle choices.

FULL-TIME STRESSORS

Monica is married, works full-time and is also the primary caretaker for two young children. When asked about circumstantial stressors, Monica says that her job is very demanding. Every day she leaves with many tasks undone and she never feels on top of her to-do list. At home, as much as she loves being a mother, she feels the same way. There is always more to do than what she can get done. She isn't sure how to prioritize. She would like to spend time with her daughters, but then dinner wouldn't get made, the house would look like a natural disaster zone, and nobody would have clean clothes. She feels anxious all the time, and even when she collapses on the couch for a 20-minute sitcom at the end of the day, her mind is racing with the things that need to be added to her to-do list.

Additionally, Monica loves her husband, but she feels irritated and resentful that he doesn't help more. When she first met him, he was a great companion, but he did not turn out to be the partner she expected for managing family and home.

Monica's circumstantial stressors are her busy job, a never-ending to-do list, and a partner who doesn't pony up. Her physical stress is lack of sleep. Her mental stress is the expectation that she needs to do all things perfectly. Her spiritual stress is that she doesn't spend as much quality time with her children as she would like, and she doesn't feel emotionally connected to her husband.

Monica's primary stress response is flight. Her constant worry is trying, albeit unsuccessfully, to help her figure out how to solve her problems or how to avoid them all together. Monica has a secondary stress response of fight when it comes to her husband. She feels resentful and irritable toward him. Hypothetically, irritation is trying to give her the power and gusto to change him.

A DIVORCE BREWING

Ed came to counseling because his wife of over 10 years told him she wanted a divorce. For him, this was seemingly out of the blue—although in retrospect, she had given him many warnings and signs. He feels angry and resentful toward her, as well as toward people in general. He becomes snappy toward others and loses his temper easily. Ed eats well and runs three times a week. He does not have any medical concerns and is physically very healthy.

Financially, he is stable and likes his job, although he has been given feedback that he intimidates others with his drive and intensity. Ed's response to their complaints is that his colleagues are lazy and unmotivated. Ed works long hours and, except for running, has few pastimes or interests.

Circumstantially, Ed is dealing with a divorce and little leisure time outside of work. Physically, Ed does not report stress. Mentally, Ed has the expectation that his wife stays married to him no matter what, and he keeps replaying this expectation in his mind. Ed also has the expectation that others work as hard as he does, and he is constantly frustrated that this expectation isn't met. Spiritually, Ed fears being alone. Ed's primary stress response is fight, and this response is hypothetically trying to give him the power to control his circumstances and fulfill his expectations.

I hope the diversity of these examples helps us understand why a "one size fits all" approach to mental health will simply never work. While medication might help someone with a biological imbalance (a physical stressor), are there other ways to address biological imbalance besides medication—such as improving sleep and nutrition? And is medication really the right approach for someone who is struggling with a circumstantial stressor such as a divorce, or a spiritual stressor such as not having a job that aligns with one's values? And while counseling may help someone with irrational expectations (a mind stressor), will it help someone whose body is suffering under the influence of a highly processed diet (a physical stressor)? And while physical supports, such as sleep and vitamins, might help one's physical response to a trauma, will it help their spiritual response?

EN SUM ...

To summarize, our negative emotions are our stress responses and they come in the form of fight responses, flight responses, and freeze responses. These stress responses are always trying to help us by identifying imbalance in our circumstances, our bodies, our minds, or our spirits. It is perfectly normal, not disordered, to experience stress responses in various forms and intensities throughout our days. But (and this is a big BUT) we need to learn how to directly identify, engage with, and transcend our stress responses, not just impulsively react to them. *Heidi, how, how, HOW do we do that?* Next chapter please ...

CHAPTER 4

WHAT THE HECK DO WE DO
WITH THESE DARN CRAPPY EMOTIONS?

Drum roll please, as we finally arrive at the key premise of this book, the point, the purpose, the good stuff, the Tootsie Roll in the middle of the lollipop, the creamy filling of the chocolate croissant, the meatball in the marinara (hmm, looks like someone needs a snack). The following is the one and only formula you'll ever need for navigating crappy emotions. Are you ready?

Soothe the body to soothe the mind. Soothe the mind to ignite the spirit.

Let me say that again, because it's a simple concept, but it's also a critical one. *Soothe the body to soothe the mind. Soothe the mind to ignite the spirit.* Okay, one more time because I'm really on a roll here, and this is my moment in the spotlight. *Soothe the body to soothe the mind. Soothe the mind to ignite the spirit.*

Yup. That was it. That's all I got. But wait, don't close the book! I promise this little formula has much more to it than originally meets the eye, and I need to say it again so that it gets stuck in your brain like bad elevator music. Soothe the body to soothe the mind. Soothe the mind to ignite the spirit.

WHY WE'RE DESPERATE FOR SOOTHING ...

Though emotions are a complex combination of our fight, flight, and freeze response—involving our circumstances, bodies, minds, and spirits—all negative emotions have something in common, and all positive emotions have something in common, at least according to one school of thought.

All positive emotions, it has been opined, can be reduced to some form of *love*. Peace is a love of the moment. Excitement is love of the imminent. Happiness can be the love of many things—circumstances, a sensory experience, a value expressed, or a goal achieved. Hope is a love of the future. Well-being is the love of self, others, and life. We could go on and on, but I'm guessing it's not too difficult to see how all positive emotions are actually various manifestations of love.

If all positive emotions are a form of love, then all negative emotions are, arguably, a form of *fear*. And while this might make sense in theory, it can be challenging to apply in practice, especially since our emotions don't necessarily *feel* like fear.

Let's break down some of the common negative emotions to make this more clear—starting with the feeling of anxiety. Anxiety has an entire spectrum of manifestations ranging from niggling worry to all-out paranoia. Any form of concern, nervousness, anxiousness, phobia, or panic is usually a fear of something bad happening, or a fear of not doing enough with our lives, or a fear of what others think of us. Since anxiety is the feeling most akin to fear, it's not too hard to identify the fear or fears driving any particular anxiety.

Depression and sadness are fairly easy to reduce to fear if you stop and really think about it. Emotions on the low mood scale—anything from feeling "blah" to being suicidal—are usually connected to the fear that there is no hope, or the fear of experiencing pain or hurt, or the fear that we are less than others, or the fear that things will never change, or the fear that everything has changed, or the fear that we're not living the right life for us, or the fear that we'll never fit in, or the fear that we're not lovable, or ...

Are you getting the idea? And the specific fear underneath a negative emotion is what gives it its nuance. For example, depression is sometimes the fear that there is no hope, while sadness is often the fear of experiencing a painful life change. Again, crappy emotions don't *feel* like fear, but they are arguably a response to a fear.

When it comes to irritation and anger, this is where finding the root of fear can be a bit tricky. Especially since irritation and anger don't feel one blasted bit like fear. They feel like being pissed off!

But if you look, and I mean really, really look, you can find that underneath the anger and irritation, there is a little tiny helpless fear that the anger is protecting. Fear of not having control. Fear of not being valued. Fear of being hurt or rejected. Fear that an expectation won't be met (this is probably the most common fear underneath anger). Fear that we made a wrong choice somewhere. Fear that we will never be happy or at peace. Fear of not being respected or respectable. Fear of our values being crossed. Fear of pain. Fear of discomfort. Fear for our safety. Fear for our loved ones or humanity or the planet. Fear, fear, fear.

On a side note, some emotions are a mixture of fear and love. Take grief for example. There is a lot of fear mixed in with grief—fear that we can't live life without someone. Fear that we will forget someone. Fear that our lives will never be the same. Fear of our own death. But there is also love in grief. Love for the person and how they touched our lives. When a person does grief work in counseling, the goal is to reduce the fear side of grief and cultivate the love part. But this can be slow work that takes time.

In learning to deal with negative emotions, it is really the fear we need to contend with, not the emotion itself.

Becoming wise about negative emotions means delving a bit more deeply into our experiences in search of the fear that an emotion is trying to protect. Finding the fear underneath a crappy emotion changes our entire perspective. It is when we get to the level of fear that we can better understand our emotions, as well as start brainstorming more meaningful responses to our problems.

Additionally, by evaluating the fear, rather than the emotion itself, we can have a better idea of the sources of emotions—circumstances, mind, body, or spirit. When the source of an emotion is our circumstances, our fears tend to be very specific about something that has happened or that very likely could happen. When we fear what others think about us, or whether we're living up to certain standards and expectations, the source of emotion is probably the mind. And when our fears are about our purpose, our intimate human connections, our values, our self-expression, or whether we are living the right life for ourselves, those emotions are coming from the spirit.

However, when an emotion is primarily due to physical imbalance in the body, I find that there is often only a vague or hazy sense of fear underneath a negative emotion. For example, I sometimes feel irritable for no reason that I can identify on weekend mornings—a time when I treat myself to an extra cup of coffee. My circumstances on weekend mornings are easy and relaxed, my mind is still groggy and beautifully quiet from sleeping, and my spirit is shouting, "Hallelujah, it's the weekend!" But my *body* is saying, "Too much bleepin' caffeine, Ol' Lady!"

Conversely, when a client presents with an oddly *bizarre* fear (such as the type of fear you think of when you hear about the disorder OCD—fear of germ contamination, fear of something bad happening if you don't turn a light switch on and off 10 times), I believe those fears also have a strong biological basis—rather than circumstantial, mental, or spiritual—that science is still trying to figure out.

When I am helping clients find the fear or fears underneath their negative emotions, if we just can't find anything specific (or just the opposite—we find something strangely irrational), then my hypothesis is that imbalance in the body—whether it be nutritional, hormonal, medical, or sleep-related—is the primary source of those emotions. This is theoretical only, as we don't have a way of scientifically assessing the primary source of emotion at this time. The good news is, the techniques in this book help with physical imbalance just as much as they help with circumstantial, mental and spiritual stress, so read on.

Going back to our original premise, crappy emotions can all be reduced to some form of fear or imbalance. Fears can come from our circumstances and are usually very specific—such as a fear of something bad happening. Fears can be generated by our minds and are usually more abstract—such as what others will think of us, or whether we can accomplish what we think we should, or whether an expectation we have is being met. Fears can come from our spirit, and these fears usually involve deeper human connection, purpose, meaning, or values. And when fear is either extremely vague or oddly irrational, physical imbalance may be at the root of things.

Regardless of where fear is coming from, however, our approach remains the same. When we experience negative emotions, we need to look for the fear underneath those negative emotions. We need to find the fear in order to—you've guessed it—SOOTHE it. And we need to soothe at the levels of mind, body and spirit.

We soothe so that we can attend to our circumstances and problems from a place of resilience.

Soothing fears is a tough concept for many of us. The mind kicks into gear and says, "What? Negative emotions don't need soothing. They need to be overcome and surmounted. And the way we overcome them is with logic or control or action."

Listen Antsy-Pants, if you are in a life-or-death situation that is immediately and clearly changeable, I give you full permission to heroically take charge and take action. But 99% of the time, when we are experiencing emotional difficulty, there is no helpful action that can be swiftly implemented. For times when our next steps are uncertain, which is *most* of the time, the starting point for negative emotions is finding and soothing the fear. And if you can't identify the fear (sometimes it's hard), that's okay, but go into soothing mode anyway. From there, you may attend to your problems, but from a resilient place, not a fear-driven one.

Think of a cute and fuzzy animal. When it is scared, what is your natural instinct? You launch into nonsensical baby babble and shift your tone to be soft and reassuring. You pet, rock, stroke, hug, or hold that puppy or kitten close. You whisper, "Shhhhh. It's okay. You're okay." You make the cute and fuzzy animal warm or surround it with something soft. You *soothe*.

This is the exact same thing that we need to do with our crappy emotions. Underneath every negative emotion is a whimpering furball of adorableness that needs soothing. But, in our world, we rarely go there. We try to talk directly to the anxiety or anger or depression with "Stop worrying already!" or "Calm down!" or "Just cheer up." Tell me, when has someone saying these things *ever* made you feel better? These words either bounce off us or make our crappy emotions even worse. And why is that exactly? My belief is because there is a fear under the negative emotion that hasn't been acknowledged or soothed.

When we find the fears underneath an emotion, we will find one of two things. One, that our fears are imagined and irrational, or two, that our fears are real and valid. Either way, the response to fear is the same. Fears need to be soothed. This is a repeater sentence. Fears need to be soothed. After fears are soothed, you can attend to your life from a more grounded place.

SOOTHING AS THE HEART OF RESILIENCE

I've heard it said that Buddhists believe there are two types of strength: "strong like oak" or "bend like grass." Both the oak tree and the blade of grass will survive a storm. In our culture, we might better call "strong like oak" *strength* and "bend like grass" *resilience*.

But, boy-oh-boy, do we ever live in a culture that sees STRENGTH as the end-all and be-all of human existence. Being strong means hardening, gritting our teeth, steeling our mind, and gutting through a challenge or difficulty. Strength is what we apply when we ask our supervisor for a raise, push through to the end of an exercise routine, tackle household tasks, stand our ground in an argument, rally for our political perspective, the list goes on. Strength is overriding pain and pushing ourselves to our limits. Strength is using sheer will to surmount challenges, surmount circumstances, surmount difficult people, surmount our own bodies and, arguably, surmount our own spirits.

Strength is when we become hard.

As a culture, we have got "strong like oak" strength mastered. We are arguably so skilled in this area, we use it most of the time for most circumstances. In fact, we're not even aware that there is an alternative to gutting through and surmounting challenge with force and fortitude.

When we experience a crappy emotion, our bodies become tense and our minds become hard. Our jaw clenches, our breath seizes, and our shoulders constrict while our internal voice rants, "You need to do better. You have to snap out of it. You've got to do something. You shouldn't feel this way. *What is wrong with you?*" Or sometimes it's, "They need to do this. They haven't done that. They've got to change. They shouldn't be that way. *What is wrong with them?*"

If you don't think you are strong, think again. You are. But there's a small problem (which is a sarcastic way of saying there's a really big problem). Using strength should be our occasional go-to. An every once in a while sort of thing for situations that we can truly change or impact. Think of a lion in the savanna. This wise beast spends the majority of its waking hours lounging in the sun eating gazelle jerky. It conserves its energy and saves its magnificent strength for when it absolutely needs it—in the heat of a hunt. As humans, while most of us can't nap under a tree all day, we should be using strength in short bursts, during critical moments, when we really need it.

Take exercise for example. A burst of tension on our muscles and our heart makes them fit. And tension in the mind in the form of a problem to solve or a lesson to learn makes the mind more vital. And a life challenge that triggers short-term suffering, such as the ending of a relationship or losing a job, can make our spirits stronger. Whilst (are you impressed with my use of "whilst"?) strength is meant to be utilized in short bursts and acute doses, our modern-day lifestyle tends to generate stressors that are experienced chronically or habitually. For this type of stress, we need resilience.

Resilience is the exact opposite of strength in that it is soft.

Resilience is when our breath eases and calms rather than seizes and intensifies. Resilience is when our bodies are flexible and free of unnecessary tension. Resilience is when we slow down rather than speed up. Resilience is when we quiet our overly rigid rules and expectations. Resilience is when we creatively adapt to or gently navigate challenges rather than fight brutally through them. Resilience is when we respond to situations with our values and our humanity rather than with force. *Resilience is what we use when we cannot instantly change or alter our circumstances (which is most of the time).* Whereas hard strength is something we need in small bursts to make concrete changes to our circumstances, soft resilience is what needs to be cultivated as a day-to-day practice.

I find it fascinating that we naturally tap into resilience for babies. When they are distressed, we instinctively go into some sort of soothing mode. We rock. We speak in soft and cadent tones. We reassure the baby or the child with, "You're okay. You're safe. It's all right." We gently shhhhh and coo. And while one might initially think that this is hooey—an indulgence just for babies—the reality is that it has a purpose. A critical purpose! The soothing and nurturing that we do for babies fosters resilience and the ability to self-soothe.

In fact, soothing and nurturing are the heart of emotional resilience. And beginning around the age of five, for reasons I will never understand, we abruptly rescind resilience, cease nurturing, and start in with the "you need to, you have to, you've got to, you should" of hard strength.

In our culture, we tend to think of resilience as weak, babyish, girlie. But resilience is at the heart of a healthy body, an eased mind, and an expressive spirit. Resilience is the core of emotional well-being. Cultivating resilience is how we navigate and eviscerate crappy emotions. Resilience is what we need to tap into when strength just plum doesn't work.

Said another way, to balance imbalance and quiet core fears, we need to learn the art of soothing. To get to a place where our behaviors and choices are determined by our spirits, not our stress responses, we need to learn the art of soothing. To make small hassles and minor triggers melt away immediately, we need to master the skill of soothing. And, in order to experience joy and love and creation, we need to keep our bodies eased, our minds quiet, and our spirits ignited. We do this so that we can attend to our lives from a calm and resilient place.

Soothe the body to soothe the mind. Soothe the mind
to ignite the spirit.

IN A NUTSHELL ...

Let's summarize everything in this book so far. Emotions are experiences, thoughts, or beliefs expressed in our bodies. Emotions are determined by our circumstances, our bodies, our minds, and our spirits. When we have positive emotions, something is going right in one or more of these areas. When we have negative emotions, there is imbalance in our circumstances, our bodies, our minds, or our spirits.

All negative emotions are manifestations of our fight, flight, or freeze stress responses. And all of our stress responses are a form of fear or imbalance. We fear things happening in our circumstances or in our world. We fear not meeting standards and expectations, whether they are our own or others'. We fear pain and being hurt. We fear change. We fear not living a life that aligns with our purpose, our values, our nature. And when the fear is extremely general or extremely irrational, we can hypothesize that the fear is from imbalance in the body. But no matter where the fear or imbalance is coming from, our response is the same. We need to soothe at the levels of body, mind, and spirit so that we may attend to our lives from a resilient place. Soothe the body to soothe the mind. Soothe the mind to ignite the spirit.

Okay Heidi, I see how you see things, but when do we learn how to soothe? Can you hurry this up a bit? Why yes, yes I can …

In this book, interventions will be divided into two categories: proactive soothing strategies and reactive soothing strategies. Proactive soothing strategies will include tips for preempting negative emotions before they ever have a chance to take hold. Proactive soothing strategies are regular practices or lifestyle choices that build healthy emotional resilience, so that stressors feel less stressful in general. Reactive soothing strategies are in-the-moment techniques for when a bad mood hits. Reactive soothing strategies take five minutes or less and can be used to contain and diffuse difficult emotions, prevent undesirable knee-jerk responses to stress, and move us more quickly toward our highest and best selves.

And the good news is that learning and implementing these soothing skills is actually pretty fun (but I'm a psychologist with a rather frightening love of cats, so my sense of fun might be warped).

CHAPTER 5

HOW DO WE PROACTIVELY SOOTHE CRAPPY EMOTIONS IN THE BODY?

We've already defined an emotion as an experience, thought, or belief expressed in the body. So if emotions reside in our bodies, doesn't it go without saying that, when it comes to addressing emotional health, we need to start with the body? A critical component of the mind-body-spirit approach to mental health involves first and foremost attending to the physical and visceral sensations of the body. To repeat: step one of our emotional health formula is to *soothe the body*.

To a certain extent, as a society, we do soothe the body when we're feeling out of sorts, but we usually do this in ineffective or unhealthy ways. For example, we eat a pint of ice cream. We pour ourselves a drink. We pop a pill. We light up a cigarette. All of these mindless habits are attempts to soothe the uncomfortable bodily markers of stress and negative emotion. And truth be told, they all work pretty well—short term. But eating and drinking our stress away is simply not sustainable long term, nor does it move us toward lasting well-being.

The good news is, I'm not going to take away your Ben & Jerry's™ or your Bota Box,® and I won't urge you to flush your Xanax® down the toilet. Instead, I'm going to ask that you start becoming aware of what you're doing when, at the end of a long day, you open that bag of chips or mix that martini. You are *soothing* the physiological effects of stress and negative emotion. But there are actually many tools available to us for soothing the body and managing emotions, especially if we learn to be creative in this realm. In the grander scheme, I want you to learn 100 *other* ways to soothe the body, so that the less healthy ones are either only the occasional go-to or perhaps not needed at all.

PROACTIVE BODY-SOOTHING STRATEGIES

Imagine, for one indulgent moment, instead of perpetually focusing on completing your never-ending to-do list, a life completely dedicated to keeping your body calm and soothed. Imagine a world where food is consumed to deeply nourish and make you feel amazing, rather than gulped on the run in a stupor. Imagine a world where our entire calendars are centered on getting quality sleep. Imagine a world where people convene not just to talk and laugh, but also to breathe soulfully, hydrate healthily, and support one another's emotional and physical health in a loving way. Imagine a world where the purpose of exercise is to vitalize and create pleasure, not to lose weight or change shape. Imagine a world where supportive and loving human touch is accessible and abundant, rather than taboo and restricted. Imagine a world where maintaining a soothed body is life's key priority.

If you stop and think about it, the world I just described is a reality for our babies and our pets. We intuitively put everything we have toward keeping them physically soothed. We nourish them, wrap them in warm things, hug and squeeze and soothingly stroke them, and go to great lengths to ensure they are loved and valued. (I have two cats, their names are Mr. Squid and Ms. Lobster, and I refuse to tell you how much money I have spent on felted wool sleep cozies, carpet-covered climbing furniture, specialized grooming brushes, bubbling water fountains, and catnip-filled kitty treats, all to keep them sated, rested, and contented.)

But when it comes to our own adult human bodies, we tend to either willfully force ourselves to eat the items our minds think we *should* eat, or conversely we grab something for convenience without mindfulness for what our bodies truly need. When we exercise, it's rarely with a sense of play, and more often with angry thoughts of, "Get thinner and more muscled, dagnabbit!" When we sleep, we think of it as an unproductive indulgence.

Rarely, if ever, do we treat our bodies with tenderness and kindness. In fact, we actually *fear* treating our bodies kindly. We fear that if we are self-loving, we will become lazy and spoiled and unlikeable and ineffectual. We believe we have to force our bodies into submission in order to "gut through" life's daily tasks. Play, nourishment, rest—bahh, that's for babies.

Please change this right now. At this very moment. For the rest of your life. Please commit to an entire future of treating your body lovingly— no matter how busy you are, no matter how much weight you want to lose or muscle you think you should gain, no matter how many ways your body disappoints you. *Treat your body lovingly.*

While we can't wave a magic wand and create Heidi's body-centered utopia, I believe all of us could do a better job of enjoying the experience of having a body—especially women. Proactive soothing strategies include anything you do to soothe and calm the body for no other reason than to soothe and calm your body. Proactive soothing strategies are not about reacting to an immediate stressor or doing damage control after a difficult event has passed. Proactive soothing strategies involve taking care of the body just for the joy of it.

Some of the following proactive habits are likely self-evident, but for some reason, we humans need to be reminded of them over and over. Others might be new or unfamiliar. All of the techniques are *loving* ways to soothe the body as part of our mind-body-spirit approach to well-being.

GET MORE SLEEP

As a psychologist, I quite often hear the following from clients: *"I sleep about six hours a night, and even though I'm a little tired, I do okay with that. I need three cups of coffee in the morning and three diet cokes in the afternoon, but I'm okay with that too. But I would like to figure out a way to access more energy and feel better. Can you help?"*

When I say, "Yes. Sleep more," I might as well be saying, "Yes, just fetch me a golden egg." Getting more sleep seems impossible, and clients usually respond to this suggestion with, "Dr. Lady, do you have any idea how much there is to DO in a day? Plus I have kids. Plus I'm more productive at night. Plus sometimes binge-watching TV or spending time on the computer just feels good. Plus when I try to sleep more I just wake up in the middle of the night and my thoughts race. Plus, in the end, I *should* be fine on six hours of sleep. Eight to ten hours is for movie stars, not me."

In the end, I do know how much there is to do in a day, I promise I do. But that doesn't change the facts. We need sleep to feel good. Maybe a few nights a year you can get away with foregoing sleep for the sake of an amazing life experience, but as a rule, we cannot access positive emotions without being rested. I'm stomping my feet and saying it again. We. Need. Sleep. To. Feel. Good. *Sleep is how the body becomes soothed.* Have you ever awakened from a really juicy nap and felt amazing? It's a rare occurrence for most of us (both the nap and the waking up feeling awesome), but that's what we're going for every day, and we need to radically alter our current mind-set about sleep. Sleep sets the stage for all emotional health, and without it, all of the other interventions suggested in this book either lose their potency or become completely ineffectual.

There have been numerous books written on the importance of sleep and how to improve the quality of it—this is not that book. But if you are having difficulty sleeping, I do suggest making the reading of those books a priority. The one area of sleep hygiene I will address is the nighttime use of electronics. This has become a big deal in our 21st century. We actually believe it's natural to respond to emails and texts, watch TV, putz on social media, or wind down with an iPad game before (and often in) bed. Believe it or not, humans happily survived their evenings without these activities for centuries before electronics even existed (yes, my dear millennial friends, there was cell-phone-free time in the dark, dreary past of human existence).

There are many problems with the use of electronics before bed, especially directly in the bedroom. Though electronic devices may allow the body to numb, they stimulate or agitate the brain. One negative email, one particularly violent TV scene, one provocative social media comment, and the mind becomes amped and alert. To boot, without even realizing it, we tend to delay our bedtime to finish that TV show (and maybe just one more episode), respond to that email (and maybe one more after that), and post our response on Facebook (and look at just one, okay maybe 10, more posts after that).

And if a boon in mental stimulation isn't enough of a reason to unplug before bed, there are mounting concerns about the neurochemical impact of the electromagnetic field and the blue light emitted by our favorite technological gadgets. I'm not going to go into the specifics of the research on this, but you have to admit, even without the science, that there is a creepy buzzy feeling when you've spent too much time staring at a screen.

Consider—both for the quality of your sleep, and as part of our "soothe the body" formula—shutting down electronics a few hours before bedtime and talking, reading, listening to music, breathing and meditating, engaging in tranquil crafts, or even just enjoying some (gasp) silence and stillness. Think of our homesteading ancestors who sat on the porch and gazed at the stars. Now *they* knew how to prep a body for sleep.

In addition to ditching electronics in the evening, I also encourage you to deeply examine that daily to-do list that cuts into your sorely needed bedtime. I know, I know—some elements of this list really, truly, indeed, absolutely, *for sure*, must be done. But many items on your list are arbitrary expectations imposed by you and/or society, and it's time to rebel. Do your children really need an activity every night of the week? How about one favorite activity a season or even twice a year? Do you really need an hour of vegging out to that television show, or can you just head straight for the mattress? Do those texts and emails really need to be responded to within the hour, or can you train your friends and family that, for the sake of health, you will not always be quick on the draw? Does your house really need to be perfect for that hypothetical drop-in guest? Or can you keep the entrance tidy and lower your standards when time is pinched?

While sleep is the physiological heart of resilience, here's the real reason I want you to spend the rest of your life cultivating your sleep hygiene. A deep slumber is one of the best natural highs that exists. Waking up from a full night's rest or a deep and juicy nap can make you downright euphoric. To boot, it's free. And we deny ourselves this fantastic sensation for the sake of what exactly? A 21st century to-do list that nobody but you really give a termite's toot about? Life has so many natural pleasures built right into it, but in our mind-driven state of "I need to, have to, got to, should," we tromp right over those pleasures and forge toward meeting the standards and expectations of the mind.

Allow sleep. Savor sleep. Heal through sleep. Let sleep be the foundation of your physical and emotional resilience.

EAT WHOLE, UNPROCESSED FOODS AND MAKE A SERIOUS EFFORT TO DITCH THE JUNK

All of us, every single one of us, know what it feels like to eat for emotional reasons. We eat when we're bored and want entertainment; we eat when we're feeling displeasure and crave pleasure; we eat to feel physically full when our days are emotionally empty; we eat to get a sugar rush when we lack natural energy; we eat to settle our anxious stomachs; we eat to be social; we eat with the goal of changing the shape of our bodies; we eat to nullify our deeper desires and dreams. Only on rare occasions do we truly eat to nourish our bodies.

Here's the good news: It's actually perfectly okay to eat to manage your emotions. Unfortunately, however, when it comes to cultivating a good mood, we tend to grab the exact opposite of what would actually help. Here's the other good news: I'm not going to vapidly suggest that you steam some broccoli the next time you're feeling anxious. You and I both know that's *never ever* going to happen. But a mind-body-spirit approach to emotional health does involve taking a long, hard look at how what you're eating impacts how you're feeling.

As you are already very aware, when it comes to eating and health, there are many contradictory and conflicting theories on what is and isn't good for you. And while many people would like a better understanding of nutrition, trying to sift through the latest research and make sense of the ever-changing theories can make you want to move to Bermuda (if you have a flight response), hide in a dark hole (if you have a freeze response), or strangle the closest available living being (if you have a fight response).

That being said, I truly believe we're starting to make headway when it comes to understanding nutrition for emotional health. Here are some of the things that, at this point, several doctors, dietitians, and nutritionists tend to agree on when it comes to food and mood. (P.S. In this book, I am going to focus more on food recommendations rather than the details of the science behind them, but I invite you to do your own research and come to your own conclusions.)

Sugar, in the amounts most of us are eating, is really, really (did I mention really?) bad.

You've already heard this. You know it to be true. But I'm saying it again. We all know sugar, particularly in the amounts found in processed and commercialized foods, hurts our bodies and destabilizes our moods. If you want to add physical stress and imbalance to your body, as well as increase your depression, anxiety, and irritability, pull through that drive-thru, or hit the bakery section of the grocery store, or get your meal out of a box or a wrapper. Even many so-called "health foods" such as sweetened yogurts, breakfast cereals, health bars, packaged diet meals, etc., have exorbitant amounts of sugar tucked sneakily in between seemingly nutritious ingredients.

Sugar spikes blood sugar levels, giving you a lovely short-term sensation of energy and euphoria. However, this fleeting high doesn't last long and, when it fades, mood and energy crash, and a feeling of crappiness takes over. So what do we do? We seek out more sugar to get us back to that feel-good place we so briefly accessed with the previous round of sugar. This leads to a never-ending cycle of hunger, overeating, volatile moods, fluctuating energy levels, and overall lethargy.

If that weren't enough, over time, our bodies become less and less resilient to sugar, resulting in a state called "insulin resistance." Insulin resistance, in one overly simple sentence, is when our fatigued cells stop responding to insulin—the hormone that helps our bodies regulate glucose (a.k.a. sugar). When our bodies reach a state of insulin resistance, our blood glucose levels remain chronically elevated, setting the stage for weight gain, brain fog, emotional volatility, inflammation, and disease.

Many people are rebelling against sugar and commercially processed foods for reasons of weight, but my stance is to cut these foods out for the sake of your brain, your energy, your stress resilience, and your emotional health. The American Heart Association recommends that we limit sugars to 25 grams a day for women and 36 grams a day for men. But, if you're like the average American, most of us, even those trying to eat "health foods," are unwittingly consuming 80 grams daily or higher. Sugary and processed foods might give you a temporary sense of "yeehaw!" but long term, they will only give you a big fat feeling of "ugghh."

Eat fat! Just make sure it's the natural, unprocessed kind.

Holy jalapeno, has the ingredient FAT ever received a bad rap for the last 60 years. As a society, we're still reeling from the era that said a low-fat diet is good for you. News flash: We've fine-tuned our science and done a 180 on natural fats. In particular, the nutritional community is singing the praises of what we call "good fats"—although what is and isn't good fat is still being reevaluated. Here's what we know for sure.

Monounsaturated fats are good. Monounsaturated fats include avocados, nuts and nut butters, seeds, olive oil, and olives. Keep in mind, monounsaturated fats are healthy only if they are unprocessed and do not have complex added ingredients or sugar. That means unsweetened almond butter and unrefined or expeller-pressed olive oil, as examples.

Monounsaturated fats improve blood flow to the brain and are associated with improved learning, memory, and mood.

Polyunsaturated fats found in fish and seafood are also universally considered good fats. Wild-caught is the most nutritious. Ethically caught is the politest. Study the seafood of your choice to learn about mercury levels and how much is safe to consume. Walnuts, sunflower seeds, and flax seeds or oil are also healthy polyunsaturated fats. Good polyunsaturated fats are high in omega-3s, and omega-3s assist with cellular communication and nerve health. When cells are lubricated and nourished, and when nerves fire smoothly, it makes it easier for the neurotransmitters associated with positive emotions, such as serotonin and GABA, to find their way into our system.

It should be noted that there are several polyunsaturated fats that are not considered good fats by some because of the manufacturing processes involved in their production. Common manufactured fats include vegetable or seed oils, margarine or other artificial sandwich spreads, commercially made mayonnaise, or vegetable shortening. Sadly, commercially processed fats are also used by most restaurants.

At first glance, these fats don't sound scary. After all, what could be wrong with vegetable oil? Or a sandwich spread that says it's heart healthy? Or that man-made shortening that makes pie crusts look so pretty and flaky? Unfortunately, processed oils and manufactured fats can be that insidious and then some. The process of fat or oil refinement involves intense heat, petroleum solvents, and chemical additives to lengthen the shelf life of the product, and I am going to strongly recommend that you avoid them. When shopping for cooking oils, look for unrefined or expeller-pressed oils. Cold-pressed oils are more expensive, but even better. Nutritionists often suggest unrefined olive oil for low-heat cooking or unrefined coconut oil (a saturated fat) for high-heat cooking.

Saturated fats such as real butter, ghee, lard, egg yolks, whole-fat dairy, fat in meat, coconut, and palm oil have been highly maligned by most of the science and literature for over half a century. However, some rogue researchers are stating that the studies against saturated fats are flawed, and when examined more closely, saturated fats might not be so evil-terrible after all.

In terms of emotional health, saturated fat is one of the raw materials of the brain, and after much reading, I personally include clean, unprocessed saturated fats on my good-fat list and eat them in mindful moderation. (This does not mean you get to go-to-town on drive-thru double cheeseburgers, however! Fast food is prepared with commercially manufactured fats and is laden with extra stuff that the body does not process well.)

Overall, fats make us feel full, and it is much easier for us to experience positive emotions when we're full vs. when we're hungry. For me, be it a placebo or real, fats make me feel calmer and more resilient shortly after eating them, and the consumption of unprocessed fat is a central focus of my diet. When you are feeling ungrounded and anxious for no reason, try eating a handful of nuts or a half of an avocado. And though it's controversial, one of my favorite go-to's when I'm feeling anxious is to eat a pat of real butter (yes, straight from the stick). It takes about 10 minutes to work, but it makes me feel sated and has a calming effect.

Do your own research and draw your own conclusions here. I realize there is a lot of fear around eating fat, and I also know that science is currently more against saturated fat than for it. However, I think that, if you delve deeper into this topic, you'll find that natural fat has been dealt a great disservice in the last 60 years, and that the real enemy is artificially processed, overly refined, or factory-produced foods.

Get some protein at every meal.

Every nutritionist and doctor agree that we need protein, but whether that protein should come from plants or animals, as well as the amounts we should be consuming, are hotly debated topics. From an emotional health perspective, protein does several positive things for mood. First, protein is full of amino acids and B vitamins, which facilitate the production of all our favorite good-mood neurotransmitters.

Additionally, protein stabilizes blood sugar. Stabilized blood sugar leads to higher energy and more even-keeled moods. I strongly recommend studying the various sources of protein, choosing the ones that work for you, and trying to get a serving of protein into every meal and most snacks. Eating protein at breakfast is especially important for boosting energy and concentration and fostering mood stability for the day.

Like fats, proteins go from helpful to harmful the more processed they are, or the more chemicals, additives, or contaminants they have in them. Additionally, for meat-eaters, consuming protein that comes from happy, grass-fed animals, rather than grain-fed factory-farmed animals, has more of the nutrients we so desperately need, and it feels better for the human spirit.

Choose high-fiber carbohydrates.

Carbohydrates are any foods that primarily break down into glucose when digested. Simple carbohydrates break down into glucose very quickly, causing blood sugar levels to spike. Most foods that come out of a box, bag, or wrapper contain simple carbohydrates. Dairy products with their fat removed and fruit juices also fall into the category of simple carbohydrates. Complex carbohydrates include vegetables, fiber-rich fruits, legumes, and whole, unrefined grains.

Complex carbohydrates have several benefits for our emotional health. Unlike simple carbohydrates, complex carbohydrates are processed more gradually by the body, helping maintain healthy blood sugar levels and stable moods. In general, the higher the natural fiber content of a carbohydrate, the more "complex" it is, and the more your blood sugar levels benefit. The fiber content of complex carbohydrates is also important for digestive health which, we are finally starting to learn, plays a critical role in neurotransmitter production and emotional health. Additionally, complex carbohydrates are an excellent source of the micronutrients we all so desperately need.

Just like fat and protein, the more processed or refined a carbohydrate is, or the more artificial ingredients it contains, the less beneficial it becomes. I know there is a lot of current excitement around low-carbohydrate diets, but if you look closely, they are primarily asking you to cut out *processed* carbohydrates such as refined grains and sugar. There isn't a diet out there that argues against carbohydrates in the form of vegetables. In fact, eating vegetables seems to be about the only thing that doctors, dietitians, and nutritionists can all agree upon.

Learn to love water. Period.

I'm sorry, it's just plain true. We need to ease up on, and ideally savor as a rare treat, the use of caffeine and alcohol. A morning cup of java isn't going to hurt most of us, but when coffee is used to get you through your day, your emotional health pays—especially if you are prone toward anxiety or irritability. You might not correlate your edginess and fatigue to that office sludge they try to call coffee, but replace it with water and you might be surprised at the changes in your energy levels and stress resilience. (Alas, this energy might not be experienced until after a short period of caffeine withdrawal, but I promise it gets easier soon!)

As for alcohol, it frazzles sleep and interferes with neurotransmitter production, both of which lead to an increase in depression, irritability, and anxiety. If you pay close attention, you *will* notice lowered resilience and mood the day after drinking, regardless of the amount.

And soda pop? It is just plain bad. Even (especially) the diet kind. There's not a single positive thing to say about it, and how it stays legal I will never understand.

In addition to scrambling some of the natural processes of the body and creating addictive habits, alcohol, soda pop, and caffeine are extremely dehydrating. If you are feeling freaked out, woefully "blah," or pissy for no reason that you can identify, dehydration might be an explanation for your crappy emotion. Think of a hangover. Dehydration in its more extreme form leaves us nonfunctioning, foggy, depressed, and physically ill.

Dehydration that is less severe may have no other noticeable symptoms other than low energy and a crappy mood.

We all know to drink a minimum of eight glasses of clean, filtered water a day for physical health (preferably out of a reusable container, not plastic), but do this for emotional well-being as well. And the next time you're feeling an afternoon slump, try guzzling some water rather than mindlessly reaching for that caffeine. Put some fruit slices in it if you want to add some bling.

Staying hydrated is more effective for energy management long term, and your mood will thank you for the choice. This advice is easy to prove for yourself. Pick one day and have a glass of water every hour, on the hour. Around dinnertime, notice your energy levels and emotional state. Boom.

Learn whether you have food intolerances or food additive sensitivities.

Food intolerances and food additive sensitivities have been a trendy topic in nutrition and health, but for good reason. We're only just beginning to understand what some common food intolerances are (wheat, dairy, corn, soy, and eggs are the main culprits), as well as the possible negative impact of certain food additives (artificial colors, sweeteners, and preservatives). The flummoxing facts about food/additive sensitivities are 1) how often they go undetected, and 2) how diverse the symptoms of food sensitivities can be—anything from problematic bathroom habits to skin problems to, wait for it, inexplicable anxiety, irritability, or depression.

For a rare handful, a change in mood is the only indication that they're experiencing a food intolerance or food additive sensitivity, so learn more about this from an expert such as a nutritionist or a naturopath, and engage in an elimination diet or conduct testing for your own food sensitivities if you have even the slightest suspicion that this applies to you.

Back to soothing the body …

I could go on, but I don't want to turn this into a diet book. I do, however, want to emphasize that examining the impact of food on mood is a big, big, big deal. More and more we're understanding that true health, including emotional health, happens when we eat naturally occurring foods instead of commercially altered ones. If you think your diet isn't impacting your emotional health, think again. The more food has been processed, refined, or commercially mucked with, the more challenging it is for our bodies to manage. This, loosely stated, creates physical stress. Physical stress triggers our stress responses. The emotional component of our stress responses is that we feel crappy. Processed foods can even be the root *cause* of your bad mood.

I personally believe that the use of whole foods for mood, rather than medication, is the future of mental health. In fact, many nutritionists will argue that anxiety and depression and irritability can not only be managed with a whole-foods diet, but they can be completely *treated* by food and nutrition. I might not go quite that far, because food does not address the other three sources of emotion (circumstances, mind, and spirit), but I will argue that a nourished body fulfills the first part of our mental health formula, which is (have you memorized it yet?) soothe the body to soothe the mind, soothe the mind to ignite the spirit.

CONSIDER NUTRITIONAL SUPPLEMENTS

I'll start this section with a disclaimer that I am not a licensed dietitian or nutritionist. Psychologists can obtain extra training on nutrition (which I have), but it is not the primary focus of our schooling. That being said, I'm a believer in the use of nutritional supplements for mental health support, and I've personally witnessed supplements provide mild to moderate (and in some fun cases dramatic) support for anxiety, irritability, and depression. This section will provide a brief overview of the supplements most researched and indicated for mental health support, but of course you should consult with a professional and do your own research before taking supplements, particularly if you are on medication or have a health condition.

Fish oil: There have been thousands of studies published on the benefits of fish oil for a plethora of physical and mental health issues, and several books have been written on this supplement alone. From an emotional health perspective, fish oil is liquid resilience for the brain. This is due to two good fats found in fish oil called EPA and DHA. EPA and DHA are the Omega-3s utilized by the brain for cellular communication. They lubricate and help everything to function more smoothly, which can go a long way to improve mood regulation and resilience. Most of us don't eat enough wild-caught fish to get therapeutic amounts of EPA and DHA, so supplementation is recommended in this area.

Quality is critical when it comes to purchasing fish oil. I hate to say it, but there are a lot of useless brands out there that, arguably, shouldn't be allowed on the market. I've heard many people complain of fish burps, and that's a sign that you have yourself a cheaply made and probably not very effective brand (it can also be a sign that your digestive system is off). Also, take your fish oil right before a meal. Many sources will recommend a specific amount of fish oil to take (usually 1200 mg), but I urge you to go by the amount of EPA and DHA in the fish oil, not the total amount of fish oil itself. Here's what I personally look for in a supplement: a mercury and pesticide free, ethically harvested, molecularly distilled, cold-sealed product (if capsules) that has 500-1000 mg of EPA and 300-700mg of DHA. (There are a wide variety of opinions on how much EPA and DHA is helpful, and these numbers are general recommendations for the maintenance of basic health. Higher doses are used in the treatment of mental health issues like bipolar disorder and ADHD, but this should be done with the help of a trained professional—usually a naturopath, a functional medicine doctor, or a nutritionist.)

Of the supplements, this will be one of the priciest, but if you can manage it, I believe it's a worthwhile emotional health investment. *P.S. If you are on blood thinners or about to have surgery, check with your doctor before starting this.*

Vitamin D: Most of us are familiar with this one. I'm just one more person casting a vote in favor of the use of vitamin D to support mood. I especially look to vitamin D when people complain of chronically low energy and winter blues. The most absorbable supplement form of vitamin D is D3. Some people have such low levels of this vitamin that medically supervised megadoses are prescribed. Get your blood levels checked annually to get a more accurate read of how much supplementation you need personally, but most of us, particularly those of us living in northern climates, could benefit from this easy and affordable supplement.

People are sometimes afraid of vitamin D because it is possible to overdose on this vitamin. However, this is extremely rare. FDA regulations suggest 600 IUs a day, but most nutritionists will tell you to consider doses around 1000 to 2000 IUs a day. I take 5000 IUs a day, but I also have my blood levels tested annually and know that this is the right amount for my woefully pallid Minnesota complexion.

Magnesium: Magnesium has sometimes been dubbed "the chill pill" of supplements. Our diets used to be naturally much higher in magnesium, but multiple factors—such as an increase in the amount of processed food consumed, as well as a depletion of this mineral in the soil—has created a deficit in our food supply. It is estimated that about 60–80% of us are experiencing magnesium deficiencies. I take 400 mg of magnesium glycinate before bed to deepen sleep. (Magnesium glycinate is a more easily absorbed form of magnesium—although it is more expensive. It's okay to use other types of magnesium, just avoid magnesium oxide as you'll pee most of this straight out. Also, be mindful of magnesium citrate because it can loosen stools—although to many of us that's a pro, not a con.)

Probiotics: Yet again, we have a topic that could be its own book. If you haven't heard of probiotics, you will. The use of probiotics to manage a wide range of health concerns has been the cornerstone of functional medicine and naturopathic health for some time, but probiotics are also becoming more recognized in the world of mainstream medicine.

What is a probiotic and why do we need it? In a nutshell, our intestines should be a rich jungle of microbes and healthy bacteria that help us digest food and absorb nutrients. This microbe-rich environment is crucial for nutrient absorption, as well as the creation of the neurotransmitter serotonin. Serotonin is the queen of the neurotransmitters when it comes to mood. We want a healthy amount of it! And while many people take an antidepressant in the hopes of optimizing the effects of this amazing neurotransmitter, the reality is that antidepressants don't create serotonin, they only help your brain use it more effectively. So if your body isn't creating a lot of serotonin due to an unhealthy digestive system, antidepressant medication isn't going to do much for you.

What causes our intestinal tracts to be so unhealthy? Alas, many modern-day phenomena. If you take or have taken medication, eat processed foods, consume sugar, drink alcohol or caffeine, use nicotine products, have an unmanaged food allergy, are chronically stressed, have a health condition, weren't breast fed, have a nutritional deficiency, are in your mature years, watch reality TV, or didn't write a thank-you note to your grandmother for that $5—you likely have a digestive system that could use a little extra support or love.

Luckily, we can help to restore intestinal health with foods rich in probiotics. You can get probiotics from fermented foods such as yogurt (ditch the brands with added sugar or artificial sweeteners and use some fruit to make it yummy instead), raw sauerkraut (unpasteurized—you'll probably need to go to a co-op and get it from the refrigerator section), kombucha, tempeh, miso, kimchi, fermented vegetables, and kefir. But if you're like many and don't eat fermented foods on a regular basis, get yourself a supplement. You're looking for one with the highest number of microbes per capsule that you can afford, preferably 50 billion, but that gets expensive. Do what you can. When I'm on a budget, I make my own sauerkraut and eat several (uncooked) spoonfuls a week as a much cheaper option …

B-Complex: A B-complex is all of the B vitamins living happily together in one capsule. Some people like to supplement with individual B vitamins (such as B12), but since all B vitamins work together, I prefer a B-complex. B vitamins are the anti-stress vitamins. They help to increase our energy and improve stress resilience and mental focus. B vitamins also aid in the production of serotonin—that neurotransmitter I blabbered on about in the probiotics section.

The rule of thumb when shopping for supplements is to look for a "B-50," meaning the product you choose should have 50 mg of the key B vitamins to be considered a quality supplement. With some supplements, such as fish oil, is often a leap of faith that the supplement is doing something good for your body, since people do not report feeling radically different when they take it. However, with a B-complex, I immediately feel a discernible boost in energy. Do take this supplement with food or you might puke. Also, it will make your urine practically glow in the dark. Clearly it's a good thing I'm not in sales, but read about B vitamins and emotional health and you'll see why it's included in this book.

Amino acids: Amino acids are natural compounds found mostly in proteins, but they can also be purchased individually as supplements. Some over-the-counter amino acids you may have heard of include 5-HTP, L-theanine, L-tryptophan, L-taurine, or GABA, to name a few. Amino acids are the chemical precursors to the neurotransmitters that help generate positive emotions. I do not feel qualified to truly explore the dosing and usage of amino acids, but I add them here because I think the use of amino acids to support mental health is a topic we'll be hearing much more about over time. I encourage you to learn more about amino acids and their impact on mental health so that you can come to your own conclusions about whether amino acid therapy is right for you.

P.S. Amino acids and medications sometimes don't mix, so if you are interested in amino acid therapy, you'll want to find a functional medicine doctor, a naturopath, a nutritionist, or a medical doctor with familiarity and training in the use of amino acids to help you find the right combination for your needs.

GET SOME LOVING MOVEMENT

We all know exercise is beneficial, but I didn't use the word "exercise," I chose the word "movement." Why? Because, for so many of us, "exercise" has become a stomach-churning word that invokes feelings of guilt, stress, and negativity. "I neeeeeed to exercise" spits out almost reflexively in conversation, and we tend to force ourselves to the gym the same way a swearing pilgrim whipped his horse through a mud patch.

Be honest for a moment—when you exercise, are you moving in a loving way? In a way that nourishes and values your body? Or are you exercising in a hateful way—trying to force your body to change? For many of us, exercise summons, at a deep level, self-loathing. In subtle and not-so-subtle ways, we exercise with an attitude of violence toward our bodies. And if the root drive to exercise comes from such a negative place, one has to ponder what that does for emotional health. Alas, exercising with a mentality of "I will *make* my body exercise," does not satisfy the first part of our "soothe the body to soothe the mind" formula.

Let's try a different approach, shall we? I've chosen the word "movement" because I want you to take this word and infuse it with love and nurturing. Movement is different than exercise because it implies listening to what your body truly needs rather than forcing it to be active in a particular way at a prescheduled time. Movement is done just for the joy of it, and not with the rigid agenda of changing our shape or weight. Movement also doesn't have to be isolated to a high-intensity workout. We move when we clean our house, walk with our friends, dance with our children, play with our pets, explore a new town, tend to our gardens—the list goes on.

Movement might be intense or it might be gentle—your body will tell you what it needs. Either way, moving to nourish and rejuvenate, and moving in a love-based way, *does* fulfill the first part of our mental health formula of soothing the body.

Once again, we can look to babies and animals as our example. Babies have energy levels that naturally peak and valley, and we allow for this.

When they need to rest, we put them down for a nap. When they're alert and full of energy, we give them space to play. We don't demand that they wake up at 5:00 a.m. to exercise for an hour before moving into their daily routines. We examine their energy first and figure out the appropriate activity for that energy second. We honor that they fluctuate between movement and energy to rest and restoration.

Only as adults do we feel the need to deny our natural energy and replace it with disciplined and methodical exercise plans. This is the mind trying to overpower the body. A loving approach to movement means tuning in deeply and listening to the needs of your body, as well as trusting that gentle movement or natural movement can be as physically and mentally beneficial as a high-impact workout at the gym. When it comes to emotional health, move in a way that makes your body feel fantastic. Move to soothe the body.

ENGAGE IN MOVING MEDITATIONS

Moving meditations are Eastern practices such as tai chi, yoga, and qigong. Luckily, we're living in a time where these forms of movement and breath are becoming increasingly popular, and the research on these practices is bursting at the seams with good news about their benefits on physical and mental health.

Moving meditations may seem like they focus on, well, movement, but the reality is that they are first and foremost *breathing practices*. Moving mediations use gentle movement to help deepen and calm the breath. It is the deepened and calmed breath that makes yogis rave about inner peace after class. It is the deep and focused breathing that stirs up insight and creativity after 20 minutes of qigong. It is the deep and focused breathing that is generating all the mental health benefits of tai chi.

The actual movement of moving meditations is quite beneficial as well. Moving meditations are noteworthy for their ability to loosen joints, stretch muscles, stimulate the lymphatic system, calm the nervous system, improve circulation, aid digestion, stimulate and cleanse the internal organs, and nourish the brain. But most importantly, these practices soothe the body, and a soothed body (as you well know at this point) is the first part of our mind-body-spirit formula for emotional health.

CULTIVATE A BREATHING PRACTICE

If your schedule simply can't accommodate a yoga or tai chi practice, there are other more convenient ways to create a breathing practice. Most of us have learned to use breath as a *reactive* tool, meaning we use breath in an effort to de-escalate an escalating emotion. That's a perfectly handy use of breath, but I will argue that breathing techniques are much more potent when they are practiced *proactively*, nipping compounding stress in the bud before it has a chance to truly manifest, and keeping lots of healthy oxygen in our bloodstream.

If you do the research, you will find that literally thousands of breathing techniques exist, most of which fall into one of three categories: stimulating techniques, calming techniques, and detoxifying techniques, (many breathing techniques do all three). I'm going to provide one breathing technique from each category, but don't limit your exploration of breathing techniques to these alone.

To cultivate a breathing practice, pick a time in your day where you can routinely commit to full and soulful breathing. I spend about five minutes breathing mindfully during my drive to work. Some clients practice breathing every time they push a shopping cart. Others do their breathing just before bed. One client even practices breathing every time he goes to the bathroom—and if that works for you, you won't hear a peep of judgment from me.

A Calming Breath: A popular calming breath that has been promoted by Dr. Andrew Weil is 4-7-8 breathing. (If you haven't heard of Dr. Weil, he is a holistic health icon and has some compelling ideas on wellness.) Dr. Weil has a short YouTube video on this breathing technique if you want to hear it straight from the horse's mouth. Here's my one-paragraph summary of his technique:

Touch your tongue to the spot where your teeth and the roof of your mouth meet. Inhale through the nose for the count of four, hold your breath for the count of seven, exhale with an audible "whoosh" sound through the mouth for the count of eight. That's one cycle. Do four cycles then return to your natural breath. After one month, work your way up to a maximum of eight cycles. If you start to feel dizzy or off, just stop. The point of this exercise is to calm and soothe the body, and if that's not happening for you, it's okay to move on to another body-soothing technique. Dr. Weil recommends doing this twice a day every day, and he emphasizes that the real benefits come after several weeks of regular practice.

A Stimulating Breath: I've heard my favorite stimulating breath referred to as "puppy-dog breath," although I'm sure there are other names out there that are fancier. I use puppy-dog breath in the afternoons when I'm starting to feel a little wilted. This is a nostril breath. Close your mouth if you're able. Set your phone timer for 15 seconds and, through the nose, breathe the quickest and most vigorous inhales and exhales you're capable of. They should be staccato and lively, and you will sound like a panting puppy-dog (albeit with mouth closed and tongue in). If you feel faint, for the love of full-coverage underwear, stop the puppy-dog breathing! But usually, this breath gives you just a little bit of a lift to get you through your afternoon. I like to do three rounds of 15 seconds each, with about a 5-10 second break in between.

A Detoxifying Breath: The breath I'm choosing for this category has the grooviest name ever—skull-shining breath. Seriously, who doesn't want to learn a breath with this name? Even a sullen teenager will think that skull-shining breath is *"like, totes hilar."* For this breath, sit with a comfortably erect spine and close your mouth if your sinuses allow. Skull-shining breath has active exhales and passive inhales, meaning you're focusing your effort on the exhales and letting the inhales happen naturally. For the detoxifying part of this breath, you are going to focus on your belly button. On every exhale, you will firmly thrust your belly button both in and slightly up, almost like an invisible set of arms is giving you the Heimlich maneuver. This will create a strong audible exhale followed by an effortless inhale.

I recommend about 10 strong breaths followed by a short break, followed by one more round of the same. This breath is designed to stir up all the stuff that hides in the deepest cavities of our lungs, so it can be powerful and uncomfortable for some. If you feel faint or sick, just stop and find another body-soothing technique. Soothing should feel good.

GIVE YOURSELF PERMISSION FOR PAMPERING

I'm sure I don't have to explain the concept of pampering in any great detail, but this includes anything "spa-like," such as massages, manicures and pedicures, Reiki, reflexology, facials, etc. Most of us don't have anything against the concept of a little pampering, but we do tend to view it as a fluffy indulgence rather than an emotional health practice. As a psychologist, I will argue that pampering does more than make your skin supple and your toes sparkle. Pampering fits neatly into our formula of, say it with me now, soothe the body to soothe the mind, soothe the mind to ignite the spirit.

LET'S STOP HERE FOR NOW ...

There are so many more things we could explore in the areas of proactively tending to our bodies, but I hope you're getting the idea. There's a reason you feel good after a massage, or an evening walk, or a deep nap, or a nourishing meal, and it's not just physical. Doing loving things for our bodies is a key element in managing our overall emotional health. *Loving our bodies cultivates resilience.*

For some reason, we have learned that we need discipline, rules, restriction, and self-loathing to be healthy. Challenge this cultural standard please. It has been very harmful to our emotional well-being, and it has disconnected us from our bodies and spirits. Start doing loving things right now. And commit to doing loving things for your body for the rest of your life. Trust that this isn't indulgent or spoiled. It's not lazy, and it's not hokey. It's resilience.

CHAPTER 6

...

HOW DO WE SOOTHE
THE BODY IN THE MOMENT?

Proactively loving the body as a way to cultivate resilience and emotional well-being probably isn't a challenging concept to buy into. And it would be lovely, wouldn't it, if we could go get a massage and attend a yoga class every time we started to feel flooded by emails, or grumpy with our partner, or overwhelmed by the news, or triggered by past traumas? But I don't know anyone whose life is flexible in this way.

That's where reactive soothing techniques come in. Reactive strategies generally take 60 seconds or less and can be implemented in the throes of experiencing a negative emotion. Reactive techniques are our go-to when we catch ourselves in the middle of negative emotions. They are designed to throw a wrench into our fight, flight, or freeze stress responses.

I want to point out that reactive body-soothing techniques are just the start of our soothing negative emotions formula. In most cases, these techniques won't alleviate strong emotions all on their own. Reactive body-soothing techniques need to be combined with the reactive mind-soothing techniques (which we'll explore later) to truly have an impact. But any time you're in the middle of a difficult emotion or experience, reactive body techniques are always the place to start.

PHYSICALLY SOFTEN

This is the technique I turn to most often as a reactive soothing technique. It's easy and effective. For this technique, simply take a moment to scan your body and see where you are unconsciously holding tension or experiencing unease, and then see if you can soften it. You might be surprised at just how much tension and unease you find. When I experience stress, I'm almost always clenching my jaw or constricting my breath, and I can easily release this tension once I'm aware of it. I also find that I often experience a vague sense of tightening in my chest and gut. While I can't physically relax these areas, I can mentally soften them, and this immediately starts to soothe the concomitant emotion.

Warning: It can be extremely difficult in the throes of irritation or anger, or any other manifestation of our fight response, to let go of physical clenching and tension. But softening is an amazing first step for bringing one back to a more grounded place where the triggering stressor can be engaged with more wisely.

I find the technique of softening beneficial in the middle of an intense discussion with my partner, Pete. When we are in a heated conversation where I know I'm definitely right and he is definitely wrong, my jaw clenches, my shoulders contract, and my breath seizes. It sometimes takes me a while to remember to physically soften my breath and body, but when I do, it dramatically changes the tone of our dialogue.

Amazingly, Pete will pick up on my shift in demeanor and he will unconsciously soften as well. At that point, we both become significantly more open to listening to one another (even though I'm still definitely right and he is definitely wrong).

Softening doesn't have to take a lot of effort—just scan your body in one big mental swoosh. If you're really intuitive, you can even scan inwardly and see if you sense tension at the level of the organs. I'm not perceptive enough to experience negative emotion in, say, my gall bladder, but I do sometimes pick up a bit of clenching in my intestines. Obviously, we can't consciously relax our internal organs, but we can use imagination and soothing breath to try to mentally soften internally.

GROUND YOURSELF

Energy workers, such as Reiki practitioners, have been telling us for eons that walking on earth or grass with bare feet is beneficial for both our physical and energetic health. I am not an energy expert or a Reiki practitioner, but I can attest that putting both feet solidly on the ground, with or without shoes, and taking a moment to mentally feel the soles of your feet, can be both rooting and soothing.

This technique can be helpful when you're sitting at a table during intense conversation, such as at a business meeting. Place both feet evenly on the ground and take a moment to feel the bottoms of your feet. If you're in a position to slip off your shoes, even better. If you can get outside and be barefoot for a few moments, that's the best. I like to use this technique when I'm with a group of people I don't know very well and am feeling socially inept. Alas, grounding does not fully prevent me from saying or doing dumb things, but it's at least a starting point for managing nerve-wracking social situations.

TAKE AT LEAST ONE BREATH

Breathing is to emotion what groans are to foot rubs. They go hand in hand. However, *in the natural order of things, an emotion comes first and then breath conforms to emotion.* Think about it. When you're anxious, what happens to your breath? It becomes short and shallow. When you're depressed? Your breath becomes feeble and erratic with weak inhales followed by shallow exhales, then some shorter inhales with long, desperate exhales. When you're irritated? You hold your breath of course. And when you're happy or peaceful or rejuvenated or in love? You breathe deeply and fully. Our emotions come first, and our breath conforms to our emotions.

The good news is, we can reverse that. If we liken emotional health to a ship, we have the ability to make our breath the captain and assign our emotion to be first mate. All that's required is noticing a negative emotion when we're in the middle of it and changing the way we breathe. If you're feeling anxious? Soften and lengthen your breath. Make it easy and pleasurable. Feeling low? Even out and vitalize your inhales and exhales. Add some energy to your breathing. When you're angry? Remind yourself to "just breathe," and allow your breath to soften you. *Every time you catch a negative emotion, soothe the breath.*

Soothing the breath will not immediately quell the negative emotion you are experiencing, but it will, at the very least, lessen the physiological impact of that emotion. To review: negative emotions are a manifestation of our stress responses and they tell us that we're experiencing fear or imbalance in either our circumstances, our bodies, our minds, or our spirits. And we've all heard at this point how stress, particularly chronic stress, is wreaking havoc on our immune systems, our cardiovascular health, our cognitive processes, our … aw heck, chronic stress is killing us. Calm breathing helps to protect our bodies from the effects of stress.

So, even if you can't change your circumstances or fully turn around your emotion, *protect your body* from that emotion by removing that emotion from your breath and making inhales soft and easy, and exhales even and full.

In addition to protecting our bodies from stress, soothing the breath in the middle of a difficult moment gives us just enough time to shift from *reacting* to situations to *responding* to them, and this is a pretty big deal. Think of some of your biggest faux pas in life—your worst blunders, your most shameful moments (we all have them). How many of them could have been waylaid if you had stopped and taken a breath? How many of the dumbest things you've ever done (and we've all done them) were more like a reflex than a conscious response? I'm willing to wager most, if not all, of our most ridiculous human moments were impulsive reactions, not thoughtful responses enacted with deep breathing and awareness.

Amazingly, the difference between a reaction and a response is one breath. One stinkin' breath. A single inhale followed by a single exhale. And though we've all heard the saying, "Less is more," in the case of breathing, "more is actually more." Two breaths are better than one, and three breaths are better than two. In a stressful situation, stopping and taking several breaths before doing or saying *anything* greatly increases your odds of a wise response rather than a dingle-headed one.

As an aside, we do sometimes need our mindless reflexes. You don't want to stop and breathe when a car veers in front of you or a child starts to walk into traffic. But those are rare exceptions, and since our reflexes naturally do kick in, we don't even really have to think about them. But when no one is in danger, take some time to soften the breath, protect your body from stress, and choose your response.

CHANGE YOUR TEMPERATURE

Changing your temperature from one extreme to another is an easy way to quickly soothe the body. If you're cool, heat up. If you're warm, cool down. Like some of the other techniques, this is something we see instinctively played out. What do we tell an angry person to do? Cool off! And we mean this literally—by taking a cold shower. What do we sometimes crave after a particularly harsh day? A hot bath to melt the stress away. Or do you want an extreme burst of excitement, euphoria, and energy? Try a polar bear plunge in a cold-weather climate.

But you don't need to immerse yourself in water to change your temperature. If it's steamy inside and frigid outside, step outside. Or vice versa. Try a hot or cold beverage. Wrap in a blanket. Shift to lighter, looser clothing. A simple shift in temperature is enough to give the entire body a bit of pleasant sensation that begins the physical de-stressing process.

RUB, TOUCH, OR WRAP YOURSELF

Yes, this is exactly as it sounds. When you catch a negative emotion, soothe the body by touching yourself (in a socially appropriate way of course!). Sometimes we do this intuitively by rubbing the back of our neck or our upper arms. Some people discreetly rub the tops of their thighs and knees. The tummy always appreciates a little rubbing. My favorite is the heart center, which is the area directly below the collar bones and over the sternum. It can be surprisingly powerful to simply place your palm over your chest when you catch a negative emotion.

If touching yourself is just too intimate (and it is for many) try wrapping yourself. If you're at home, use a blanket. In public, women are able to wrap themselves in a cardigan or a shawl. Wrapping is tougher for men socially.

I find it interesting that we automatically use touch to soothe babies or pets, but we find it corny or inappropriate to do the same for ourselves. Using soothing touch is one of my instant go-to's, along with softening my breath and body. I hold my own hand discreetly under the table or bring it to my heart center when I am alone. And when seated, you will often see me hugging myself as though I am the most adorable teddy bear I have ever encountered. If you are giggling or rolling your eyes, I understand. But perhaps ask yourself why self-soothing is so uncomfortable and whether it really needs to be?

BALANCE YOUR BLOOD SUGAR

I have already discussed the general mental health benefits of proactively eating whole foods, particularly clean proteins, unprocessed fats, and high-fiber carbohydrates, but food can also be a very effective *reactive* mood-soothing technique. It's actually okay to "eat your emotions." However, our instincts, when stressed, are to turn toward simple carbohydrates, usually something sugary or salty. Instead, I encourage you to reach for a snack that combines a protein with a good fat. Examples include deli turkey slices and a small avocado, or almond butter mixed with chocolate protein powder, or some hard-boiled eggs mashed with safflower mayo (this is a good-fat mayo), or some olives and a few slices of nitrate-free salami.

In an ideal world, we would eat a balance of proteins, fats, and complex carbohydrates, but our modern-day diet tends to be simple carbohydrate heavy, which can negatively impact blood sugar levels. The purpose of eating a protein and a good fat is to balance blood sugar levels, which leads to a more balanced mood and higher stress resilience. You are welcome to add a high-fiber carbohydrate to this technique in the form of vegetables or whole grains, but my warning here is to watch that your carbohydrate choice doesn't outweigh your protein and fat choices.

Fat satiates and protein helps maintain consistent energy levels. Combining the two can be an effective and satisfying way to soothe the body relatively quickly. As mentioned, my guilty pleasure for soothing is a prodigious pat of butter! And then I scrounge around for whatever protein I can find to pair with it. I'm not saying you necessarily need to do the same, but find a way to make it fun.

USE A DRY BODY BRUSH

A dry body brush is an inexpensive tool that can be found online or in the health/beauty section of some stores. It's a natural bristle brush, about the size of the palm of your hand, designed to exfoliate the skin. I keep a dry body brush next to my sofa in my living room. If I am feeling out of sorts, I put on a loose bathrobe and use the brush on my bare arms, legs and belly.

If my mood is a bit more anxious, I use the brush in a gentle and calming way. However, if I am low on energy and crave a little vitality, I use the brush more quickly and vigorously to wake myself up. Using a dry brush stimulates or calms your nervous system depending on the intensity you choose. The dry brush has the added perk of making your skin rosy and soft, but that's beside the point ...

SMELL SOMETHING YUMMY

This one is simple. Yummy smells facilitate yummy moods. Yummy smells soothe the body. Smelling aromatic things also sneakily leads to deep breathing, so this is a two-for-one soothing technique. There are many out there who practice something called aromatherapy, where scents are very conscientiously selected for their various healing properties and soothing characteristics. This is an interesting field, but for the purposes of emotional resilience, aromatherapy can be simplified: smell good things and breathe deeply when you do.

LOOK TO THE HORIZON

When we are in distress, our eyes tend to dart from object to object, and we limit our gaze to a few inches around us. You can sometimes tell when a person is experiencing a crappy emotion because they won't look you in the eye, and they send their gaze downward or move their eyes rapidly about. Extending your gaze to the horizon and focusing on one point is an easy way to start the physical soothing process.

MOVE FOR ONE MINUTE

We sometimes avoid movement as a reactive soothing strategy because we assume we need an entire workout in order for it to be effective. Setting a timer for one to three minutes and stretching, bouncing, twisting, or walking up and down stairs can be more than enough to soothe the body. Try it and see for yourself.

IN SUMMARY

While strength requires hardening the body and steeling the mind, *resilience* involves softening and soothing the body. Reactive body techniques improve emotional resiliency and begin the calming process. Reactive body techniques also increase your chances of not doing something cotton-brained in the face of stress.

But mostly, reactive body techniques lay the foundation for the real work, which is soothing the mind. There are countless ways to soothe the body in a stressful moment, and hopefully reading this chapter has you brainstorming a few healthy and simple ideas of your own. No matter how you go about it, cultivating the habit of soothing the body sets the stage for the next chapters of this book, where the techniques really *can* lead to dramatic emotional shifts.

CHAPTER 7

...

HOW DO WE PROACTIVELY SOOTHE CRAPPY EMOTIONS IN THE MIND?

Quick, tell me five ways to soothe the mind ...

I'm waiting.

Okay, obviously we aren't talking directly and I will never get to know if you were able to do this, but if I had asked you five ways to soothe the body, that probably would have been a much easier question to answer than five ways to soothe the mind. We've already discussed the fact that, as a society, we tend to calm our bodies with food and alcohol. But we do not have a culturally condoned formula for calming our minds.

When I ask at workshops what we do to calm our minds, the response I usually receive is, "We watch TV." And while there is nothing wrong with enjoying television now and again (I'm a sap for *The Bachelor* myself— don't judge!), TV is more of a mind-*numbing* technique than a mind-soothing one. And sometimes, especially if you are a news junkie or like shows with violence and thrills, TV is actually a mind-*agitating* activity rather than a mind-soothing one.

Besides TV, we try to soothe the mind by distracting and staying busy—whether we hang with friends, or putz about the house, or care for our children and pets. Again, there is nothing wrong with any of these activities, and distraction can be helpful at times. However, we need to be mindful of the way in which we distract, because we can end up creating more stress than relieving it. For example, if we hang out with friends who frazzle us more than soothe us, then socialization is not an effective mind-soothing technique. Or, if we putz around the house and end up creating even more to-do list items for the mind to puff up about, this is not an effective use of distraction. In order to be effective, mind-soothing techniques require a conscious effort to ease and nurture the mind.

So what do we do to consciously soothe the mind? This is where we're going to be spending the bulk of our exploration, because if you are 1) a human who 2) has a mind, then you know that the mind is far from a soothed or relaxed entity. Those who study mindfulness call the day-to-day nature of our minds: "monkey mind." I think this is an understatement. My mind is more like a posse of chest-beating gorillas scarfing Skittles, learning to hip-hop dance in a blizzard. It's chaos up there! Thoughts are being generated at light-speed rates, usually more than one at a time. And these thoughts are a sloppy mix of helpful, neutral, not helpful, judging, reasonable, unreasonable, encouraging, discouraging and weird. To make matters worse, the endless stream of thoughts in our heads distracts us from our deeper spirit. Every time we are lost in thinking (which is often), the mind is ruling the roost and the spirit gets drowned in the noise.

Think about it for a moment, when do you feel like your best self? Usually it is directly after an activity that has quieted the mind, like a yoga class, or a really good nap, or a period of time spent in prayer, or an indulgently steamy shower. When we quiet and soothe the mind, we make room for creativity, insight, vitality, and intimacy. This is a good place to remind you of our mental health formula. Sing it loud for me please: *Soothe the body to soothe the mind. Soothe the mind to ignite the spirit.*

PROACTIVE WAYS TO SOOTHE THE MIND

Here's the good news. All of the proactive body-soothing techniques we read about earlier apply to this chapter as well. When we proactively soothe the body, we *automatically* start to soothe the mind without any conscious exertion whatsoever. A calm and soothed body sets the stage for a calm and soothed mind. But there are also proactive mind techniques that go beyond the soothing offered by the body-soothing techniques. Proactive mind-soothing techniques take our soothing one step further.

SEATED MEDITATION

Even if you live under a rock, you've heard of meditation and the growing interest in this. Meditation is a mind-calming practice that is as ancient as dinosaur doo. We have already looked at *moving* meditations in our body-soothing techniques section. But there are also several types of meditation that are not physically engaging. They generally involve being seated on a cushion or a chair. Sometimes they are conducted lying down. I am separating the non moving meditations and including them in this section of the book, since seated meditations tend to focus directly on soothing the mind.

If you are already familiar with meditation, you can skip to the next section, but if meditation has never been fully explained to you, let me do the honor now. It's not the big magical mystery people sometimes think it is. Meditation, all forms of it, share the following three components:

First, all meditations have something on which we're focusing our attention. This is called our "object of meditation." Usually, the object of meditation is our breath, simply because breath is ever present, pleasant and effective. I also think breath is used because it naturally calms the body, which helps to soothe the mind. But there are lots of other possible objects of meditation—prayer beads, a candle flame, a soothing phrase or sound, a visualization, a contemplation, the five senses ... the list goes on and on. The object of meditation doesn't have to be anything fancy. In fact, a common meditation uses a raisin as the object of focus. You just have to find *something* to focus on.

Second, all meditations have a *type* of attention. We don't generally think of attention as having a particular bias or quality, but boy-oh-boy does it ever. And the nature of our attention can wreak havoc on how we experience life and the emotions that we generate. Think of driving. Some people drive with a "white knuckled" sort of attention. Quite literally, they grip the steering wheel, lean forward, squint their eyes, tense their shoulders, and hyper-focus on what's happening directly in front of them (I'm like this, truth be told). They are certainly paying attention to their driving, but the type of attention they are using comes with an emotional cost—anxiety or anger.

Then there's the way my partner Pete drives. He places one knee on the steering wheel to free up his hands and appears to be looking at everything but the road. Simultaneously, he somehow manages to eat a donut, drink coffee, tell me every detail of his week, and pick the lint out of his belly button, all while miraculously getting to his destination. He is also using a particular type of attention—an attention that is unfocused and redirected by whatever moves, sparkles, makes a noise, or is covered in sugared sprinkles.

In our own lives, we likely switch back and forth between white-knuckled attention and partner-Pete attention. We focus in an anxious way one moment, and then our attention wanders aimlessly the next. Then we find something else that captures our concentration for a bit, and then we return to spitzing and sputtering about.

But there is another option. Attention can be soft instead of hypervigilant or haphazard. Attention can be loving instead of critical or careless. Attention can be easy and gentle rather than intense or scattered. Attention can be curious rather than judging or unfocused. And this is the type of attention cultivated in meditation—soft, loving, curious, and calm attention. This type of attention is often called "mindfulness," and meditation is the practice of cultivating mindfulness. The great thing is, when we pay attention to things in a soft and gentle way, we set ourselves up to:

- be more productive and waste less time and energy with anxiety or lack of focus
- see things more clearly and fully

- feel calmer and wiser
- respond to the situation at hand with our values rather than our impulsive reactions

Think of any Asian kung fu film you've ever seen where the solitary ninja is about to be attacked by a gang of bad-guy bandits. The ninja doesn't scream and yell and flail and cry (that's the haphazard type of attention). He also doesn't become overly tense and hyper-focused on just one bad guy (that's white knuckled). He takes a deep breath, softens his eyes, softens into his fighting stance, and uses a soft attention to attend to the whole team of tyrants one "hi-ya" at a time. He is using mindfulness.

Finally, all meditations involve a commitment to disengaging from the thoughts and stories that keep us caught up in our heads. And though this might not sound like a big deal, the ability to separate one's self from one's thoughts is a really groovy thing when you stop and think about it. After all, we are in our heads *all day long*. Our thoughts are what we focus on *more than anything else*—certainly more than our bodies and spirits, and usually more than our current lived experience. But, when we stop and breathe, we see that there is a part of us that is separate from our thoughts—a part that can step back and observe the mind the same way a coach can study a game from the sidelines. Meditation teaches us how to gently peel away from the destructive or habitual or wheel-spinning thinking of the mind and move us toward a deeper place of spirit. Said another way, meditation soothes the mind so that spirit can be accessed.

I'm going to be candid. I have studied traditional meditation, tried all sorts of seated and supine meditation techniques, even taught meditation, but it is not my favorite mind-soothing practice. In fact, of all the mind-soothing techniques, it's my personal least favorite. I say this only to have a sisterly moment with others who have tried, and seemingly failed, to attach to a meditation practice. Meditation is good, don't get me wrong. It's actually very, very, very good. But it is not the only mind-soothing technique, even though it is sometimes exalted as such. So, if you don't like meditation, don't fret. There are alternatives.

NATURE

Sigh. Even just hearing the word begins the mind-calming process. It doesn't take a psychologist to tell you that the beauty found in nature is our planet's intended form of Prozac®. When we experience the awe or beauty of our natural world, our bodies lighten and our minds become easier. Nature soothes the mind. Nature helps us access the spirit.

I used to live in Alaska, and I can still remember how a glimpse of the mountains in the fading sun would instantly cleanse me of my worries and make me feel grateful to be alive. When we protect and preserve the environment, we're not just saving the planet, we're fostering our own emotional health. Nature is a critical component of mind-body-spirit vitality. Finding more ways to spend time in nature—even if it's just sitting next to a window and listening to the birds—is an excellent way to proactively keep the mind from spiraling out of control. Nature wakes up the spirit in a magical way.

MUSIC

When I asked what soothes the mind, some of you probably thought of music right away. Soul-inspiring music can instantly quiet the mind and connect us to our deeper selves. Conversely, really bad music can stress the body, and agitate the mind and spirit.

For some of us, choosing and listening to music is a deliberate part of our days, but for many of us, music is something that happens in the background of our lives in the car, on elevators, or in waiting rooms or stores. We do not always consciously choose what we listen to and how we're engaging with it. Are you selecting inspiring music on your drive to work, or are you haphazardly hearing whatever is on the radio in a way that frazzles and stresses? Are you actively listening to and humming along with music with your children at night, or are you numbing to television instead? When you splurge on a night out, does it include well-selected live music and the mind-soothing energy that goes with it? Or are you picking outings that are noisy in a way that disturbs rather than ignites?

The conscious use of music, like nature, is a powerful mind-soothing technique that can tame our inner monkey mind and connect us to something deeper. By the way, soothing the mind doesn't necessarily mean slow, soft music. Choosing music for emotional resilience means choosing whatever music shuts up the dialogue in your head, while at the same time igniting your spirit.

THE CREATIVE ARTS

Along with music, all creative arts have the potential to soothe the mind and ignite the spirit. Different areas of creativity speak to different spirits in different ways. For some, the form of creativity that enlivens them might be fashion, for others the written word, for others the perfect culinary experience, and for others the unique architectural design of a well-crafted building.

I shudder to think of a world where the creative arts are marginalized or considered inconsequential (oh wait …). In our modern world, the creative arts, which come from a place of spirit, are often placed on the back burner in lieu of the demands of the mind. The mind wants productivity and logic and efficiency, and as we all know, the creative arts are anything but productive or logical or efficient.

However, from an emotional health perspective, the creative arts are extremely vital to the mind-body-spirit connection. Whether it be paintings, photographs, fashion, theater, poetry, music, craftwork, you name it—the creative arts capture our attention and quiet that doggone spinning-hose of a mind. And when we connect with something creative that speaks deeply to us, our spirit is awakened. Appreciating creativity in any form is an excellent, proactive mind-soothing technique.

ENGAGE IN THE CREATIVE PROCESS

Not only does enjoying the creative fruits of others instantly vitalize the soul, *being* creative is also an express route to spirituality. And please do not confuse being creative with being talented or skilled or perfect. Planning a themed dinner party, cleaning your closet and putting together tops and bottoms in new ways, writing an ode to your sweetie, trying new recipes, coloring with crayons—anything that engages the imagination is an excellent way to soothe the mind and access the spirit.

As a side note, getting the creative juices flowing is one of my favorite interventions for depression, but there's a catch. You can't put pressure on yourself to actually *do* something creative, but you can *scheme* something creative. If you are an entertainer too depressed to entertain, lay on the couch and start daydreaming about the party you will throw when you do have energy. If you are a singer too depressed to sing, sing in your mind or look up songs on the internet that you want to eventually perform when you are no longer depressed. If you are a crafter too tired to craft, get on Pinterest and look at pictures of what you want to do once you do have the energy.

The simple act of daydreaming or planning your creative projects can have as much of a spiritual benefit as actually engaging in these activities directly. (Often, the mind wants to get involved in the creative process instead of the spirit. And the mind will say judging things like, "You can't do that. It's too much work and there are so many ways you'll screw it up and make it not perfect." Gently tell the mind that it's out of turn. Creativity is the realm of the spirit and no stupid, bullying mind is allowed).

EMOTIONAL INTIMACY

We've addressed meditation, nature, and anything and everything related to creativity as ways to quiet the mind and access the spirit, but what else? You probably read the subheading and know the answer here. Emotional intimacy. Not just lighthearted human connection, but deeper emotional intimacy, and it's important to distinguish what this is.

I'm afraid our culture has become a little confused about how to truly connect with others, as we currently try to establish intimacy by being impressive. We are raised to believe that being impressive is 100% good, and that it's what we should strive for. We should impress our relatives with our grades and our neighbors with the sports team's winning streak. We should impress our friends with our perfect home or our latest achievement. We should impress our supervisors with our productivity. We should impress new acquaintances with our wit and intelligence. We should impress our Instagram friends with a picture of our latest vacation. I could go on and on and on. We think that being impressive and connecting with others are pretty much one and the same, and in order for others to like us, we assume we have to figure out some way or another to be impressive.

But here's the problem, being impressive has one of three results: 1) sometimes being impressive entertains others, 2) sometimes being impressive annoys or alienate others, 3) sometimes being impressive, well, impresses others. But one thing being impressive will never do is make us feel close and connected to others.

Intimacy is different from being impressive, and it requires three ingredients. Ingredient one: a minimum of two people. Ingredient two: one person being authentic and vulnerable. Ingredient three: the other person receiving that vulnerability nonjudgmentally. Let me say that another way. Intimacy is one person sharing something true and personal (something that is likely *not* impressive) and another person receiving that vulnerability with understanding and compassion. Let me say that another way. Intimacy is one person communicating from a place of spirit and the other person receiving from a place of spirit.

Think about a time you felt especially close to someone. Were one or both of you being impressive? Were you dazzling someone or being bedazzled? Or was one person genuinely sharing something vulnerable or difficult or weak, while the other one listened? When we want to feel close to someone, we need to risk exposing our authentic selves rather than trying to impress, and we need our vulnerability to be heard nonjudgmentally. Conversely, we need to listen to someone else non-judgmentally while they risk vulnerability and authenticity. *This* is how we connect more deeply as humans. When we are intimate, our mind and bodies automatically quiet, and we are directly connected to the spirit.

True intimacy can be incredibly difficult to find, and if it is not available in your life right now, don't panic. There are other ways to feel alive and connect to our higher selves. But also don't give up your search for friends or partners who understand and are capable of emotional intimacy. They're out there.

IN SUMMARY

Now that you have a sense of this, you might be able to find other ways to quiet the mind that weren't explored in this chapter. But, in a nutshell (here comes the highlight-able summary statement for this section), proactively soothe your mind with meditation, nature, music, the creative arts, and emotional intimacy. Do as much of this as possible for the rest of your life. It's good for you.

CHAPTER 8

■ ■ ■

HOW DO WE SOOTHE THE MIND IN THE MOMENT?

You're here! You've arrived at the most important part. This chapter is the (humanely raised) meat and (organic) potatoes of this book. It's where the va-va meets the vroom. Where the cat gets to meow, and the plus-sized woman gets to sing … okay I'll stop now. But the point of all this hullabaloo is to celebrate this very important chapter.

Why so important? Well, reactive mind techniques are what we're all desperately craving when it comes to navigating challenging emotions. These soothing techniques can be applied in the moment of stress as a way to immediately increase resilience. Unlike the proactive mind-soothing techniques, these reactive ones do not require planning and time. Most of them can be done in a few minutes or less. I'm going to start with the simplest tools and work my way up in complexity.

"SHHHH … "

When you are in a heated emotional moment, sometimes the simplest way to quickly quiet the mind is with a gentle (emphasis on the word *gentle*) "shhhh." This sound can either be created silently in your mind or whispered audibly. Why is it helpful? "Shhh" is the human-generated form of white noise, and white noise is soothing both mentally and biologically. There's a reason we use this sound with babies, and directing this white noise toward ourselves has the same effect.

Now let's get real here. Saying "shhh" to yourself is not going to dramatically solve your problems or magically shift your mood. But it does make it a wee bit harder for the "need to, have to, got to, shoulds" of the mind to take over.

Furthermore, making a "shhh" sound involves our breath in a more conscious manner, which has the added benefit of calming us physically. And, as you well know at this point, we soothe the body to soothe the mind, and we soothe the mind to ignite the spirit. Using a "shhh" for a short period of time (longer if the situation is more intense) can help calm both body and mind just enough so that the spirit can get in the mix.

SING YOUR THOUGHTS

This is a playful, reactive, mind-soothing technique. I like to use this one in situations where I am mildly irritated but also helpless to change anything. Singing your thoughts is exactly like it sounds. First, pick a tune. It should be something light and playful (using Bjork would not work for this technique), and mentally sing your thoughts to that tune.

Let me give you an example. My go-to tune is "I'm a Little Teapot." Just before writing this section of the book, I was waiting in a rather long line at a coffee shop. It was a busy time of morning to begin with, but the line was substantially slowed by a woman ordering very particular lattes for her entire office. I found myself getting quite annoyed (remember, I have a fight response toward stress). So I used the sing-your-thoughts technique to temper my emotion and it went like this (to the tune of "I'm a Little Teapot"):

This woman in line is a pain in the petunia.
Why is her stupid list of coffees so long?
Can't she see that she's ruining everyone's morning,
I want to her to shut up, shut up, shut up.

Now one of two things happen with this technique, and they're both positive. Either 1) I vent enough that I don't end up doing something regretful like kicking her in the shin, or 2) I end up laughing at myself for singing like a four-year-old. It's a win/win.

As a side note, I need to emphasize that this technique is to be done *silently*. I had one wonderful client misunderstand the instructions and sing her song aloud to her teenage children when they were being annoying. I'm making up her tune, but I'm guessing it went something like this:

You two are driving me absolutely crazy.
Some days I wonder what it's all for.
I'm going to get a bottle of wine and drink it all up,
And it's all your fault just so you know.

She said her children looked at her aghast and said, "Mom, what are you doing?" Then they all burst out laughing. Singing her thoughts shifted the whole mood of the room. Now, as a joke, her children will start playfully singing their frustrations aloud, and the technique has turned into a lighthearted way for family members to vent. In fact, I take back what I originally said about using this technique silently. Try it out loud when you feel like having some fun!

SHIFT TO A NURTURING INNER NARRATOR

When it comes to our inner world, all of us have what I like to refer to as "the inner narrator," which is a voice (or sometimes a committee of voices) that blabbers in our head all day long. This helps us navigate everything that happens in a day. It keeps us on task. It allows us to negotiate social situations, brainstorm solutions to problems, and know what is right and what is wrong (and who is right and who is wrong).

While we don't really pay much attention to the tone and attitude of our inner voice, the reality is, this voice that guides us throughout the day is *not neutral at all*. It has opinions and an attitude. And for many of us in this culture, our inner voice sounds something like a coach. It tells us to get up and get going, no time to waste! It tells us we need to do more, be more, accomplish more, achieve more, acquire more, work harder, get fitter, because life is about achieving and obtaining and doing! "Go, team, go," shouts the voice.

Having this coach as our inner narrator is perfectly acceptable *when we are in a neutral or positive place*. In fact, cultivating the voice of the coach is what motivational books tend to focus on, and an entire field of mental health called "Life Coaching" has developed around this concept. As a culture, we really value the coaching model and we use it in our businesses, our athletics, and our politics.

But there's a small problem, which as you know by this point is a sarcastic way of saying it's a really *big* problem. The coach voice works when we're in a positive place emotionally, but it doesn't work when we're feeling low. When we are experiencing any form of irritation, anxiety, or depression, what we hear is no longer the voice of a loving, motivational coach. Instead, the voice becomes the bully, the drill sergeant, or the critic. When we're in a negative place emotionally, our inner narrator adds an unspoken ending to its command: Get up and get going *or you are a lazy, useless slob*. Work harder and accomplish more *because you are a failure if you don't*. Be more and be better *because you are a loser just as you are*. No matter how much we're doing, the bully, the drill sergeant, and the critic tell us that we could and should be doing more; that we are on the verge of utter failure. The bully, the drill sergeant, and the critic tell us we need to be constantly striving to have any worth or value as a human. The result is an unrelenting undercurrent of shame and disappointment. We feel like we're letting ourselves and others down.

Instead, I would like us to consider an alternative inner narrator: the nurturer. A nurturing narrator talks to us in a soothing and loving way. It tells us it's okay to work hard, but we need healing and restoration, too. A nurturing narrator reassures us that we're going to be okay no matter what, that it's okay to be human and make mistakes. It encourages us to trust in ourselves and follow our hearts.

Unfortunately, most of us rarely access the nurturer because we've learned somehow that this voice is corny or weak or selfish, or in the words of one of my clients, "It's wussy." We fear that if we are nurturing and encouraging, then we are somehow deluding ourselves. We fear that we will lose all motivation if we don't bully, drive, or force ourselves to attend to our to-do lists.

Nothing could be further from the truth: Nurturing is one of the core ingredients of emotional resilience. When we nurture ourselves or others, we foster inner strength. Nurturing is how we fuel ourselves during difficult times. When we fail to nurture ourselves and only try to surmount difficulty with brute force, it's like trying to drive a car without oil. It eventually seizes up and shuts down. We become sick, or numb, or depleted, or disconnected from vitality.

Instinctively, we know that our inner world needs nurturing. For example, when a baby cries or becomes frustrated, we don't go into drill sergeant mode. We go into nurturing mode: we "shhhh," we rock, we soothe, we tell the baby that everything is going to be okay. We don't consider this talk weak or pitying, so why do we think differently when it's directed at an adult? We shouldn't. A soothing tone is nature's ointment for emotional challenge. Nurturing fuels us inwardly. It's what negative emotions need in order to quiet and calm and make room for action.

There is still room for "the tough coach" too, but that voice is only effective once we are already filled and fortified with all the resilience of the nurturer. In fact, if you look at truly great coaches, they start with a nurturing tone when their team's morale is low, and *then* they transition toward the more motivational "go, team, go" voice of the classic coach.

In a perfect world, the voice in our heads would be whispering soothing, sweet nothings into our minds all day long. "Shhhhhh. You've got this. It's okay that such-and-such scares you. It's understandable that you feel that way. Slow down and go easy. Believe in yourself. You're doing a good job. One step at a time," and so on and so forth. If the nurturer were to guide us throughout our day, every day, day after day, our inner worlds would become quieter, calmer, more nourished, more flexible, and more resilient.

This is an area where I really practice what I preach. I would sound pretty silly to most if my inner narrator were audible (and sometimes it is when I'm home alone). My self-talk often resembles a scene from *Cinderella*, where she's singing with the birds and sewing booties for talking mice. I sweetly talk to myself as though I were my own child. This is not 24/7 around the clock, because I forget and have to keep remembering to turn it on. But I do it at least once every day. And I believe that, as a result of this self-nurturing practice, I am much quicker to soothe and recover during a truly difficult situation.

Let me give you an example. In the winter of 2016, I was heading to an early yoga class across town. It had snowed heavily the night before, and the roads were pretty slippery. I drove slowly and cautiously, but as I exited from the main highway, my car started to fishtail. Now, 10 years prior to the writing of this book, I would have screamed an expletive that cannot be printed, white-knuckled the steering wheel, and wet myself a little bit. But because I had been practicing my nurturing narrator for many years, I was amazed to see it kick right into gear. As the car swayed back and forth, I heard a voice say, "Shhhh, you've got this. Breathe. Turn into it." Self-nurturing was my visceral response to a crisis situation, and it happened to be a very helpful response. It was also proof to me that self-nurturing has a deeper internal effect over time.

Let's look at a playful example of what happens when you take nurturing self-talk to an extreme. Nathan worked at an emotionally draining job dealing with disgruntled clients in his company's customer service department. He usually left work feeling depleted and a bit beat up emotionally. When he arrived home, his 6-year-old son was always eagerly awaiting him. Though Nathan clearly adored his son, he found that because he was so drained from work, everything his son did (being noisy, making a mess, demanding attention) would immediately irritate him. To make matters worse, he immediately felt guilty about his grumpiness, and his inner dialogue became critical and self-depreciating: "What is *wrong* with me? Why can't I just enjoy my time with my son like a normal father?" Alas, this self-talk would only deplete Nathan further.

In reality, Nathan's irritation was only his fight response trying to give him a little power to get through the evening. Having compassion and respect for his emotion, rather than judgment, was the first focus of our therapy. Then, Nathan and I decided that, to break this emotional cycle, Nathan needed to cultivate an emotional restoration practice on his way home from work. This practice involved Nathan taking at least five minutes of his drive to talk to himself the same way he talked to his son when he was a baby. I encouraged him to be over the top in his dialogue.

Here is a sample of the self-talk I recommended to Nathan. Brace yourself, because it sounds extremely corny when we're in an intellectual place, but it has an entirely different impact when we're in a negative emotional state: "Shhhh. You're okay, Nathan. You're safe and free now. You've got this life stuff, kiddo. Being all grown up ain't easy, but you are doing a really good job, Nathan. In fact, you're actually pretty darn amazing. Who's such an amazing guy? Nathan is!"

Yes, I know how this sounds and I can see you rolling your eyes. But let's not forget, *nurturing soothes the mind and a soothed mind is a resilient one.* It's only our cultural learning that makes nurturing seem trite. In reality, nurturing is crucial to emotional well-being.

When we discussed this technique, Nathan told me that this is the way he used to talk to his Labrador puppy, so we started calling this practice "puppy time." Nathan shared that he felt pretty ridiculous the first several times he used "puppy time." But with time and practice, he discovered that the more he got into it, the more he found himself laughing out loud and pulling into his driveway refueled and ready to hug his son.

You'll remember in Chapter 5 how I stomped my feet and asked us to commit to doing loving things for our bodies, in the name of physical and mental health. Well, this is my corresponding foot-stompin' advice for the mind: *Commit to the practice of cultivating a nurturing inner voice for the rest of your life.* If I were to run for president, my platform would be that we shift the nature and tone of our inner voices (I would also argue for three-day workweeks and free dark chocolate for everyone).

Imagine a planet where people were internally cooing and reassuring and nurturing. How would this impact our spirits and our bodies? How much better would we treat others? How would we navigate (individual and collective) challenges differently if we were coming from this core of self-kindness?

CHALLENGE THE FEAR

For those of you who just can't wrap your (drill sergeant) minds around the use of radical self-nurturing, I offer you this: Find the fear underneath your negative emotion and think of it as the opposing football team angrily barreling your way at 100 mph and fight back! But don't fight the situation or person at hand, at least not initially. *Fight the fear.* Fighting the fear is what makes the difference. And do it in a loving way, not a self-deprecating one. After all, you are strong and powerful. You are not going to be dominated by some schmarmy, piss-ant fear, darn it. Stand tall. Rally. Face that fear. Then intercept the ball and run for an unexpected touchdown. Rah, rah, rah! (I am not a sports person, so I have no idea if that even made sense.)

Let me give you an example of how this works. I have fears about my weight. I'm healthy and active, but I have a build that is never going to make the cover of a magazine or make jaws drop in a two-piece. Thinking about weight makes me anxious, and I know the underlying fear is that others won't find me attractive. For whatever reason, self-nurturing doesn't quite work for me with this particular fear. When it comes to body-image issues, I find that challenging and rallying against the fear (and not my body!) is more effective than the nurturing approach. "Heidi Kopacek, you belong in this world and are full of life. Let that radiate, sister! Stand strong and proud. Love yourself and let others love you. Demand your place in the world. Go team Heidi, go! Roar!"

In most cases, I still believe that nurturing and soothing fear is more effective—not to mention desperately needed by our spirits. But if you just can't bring yourself to that nurturing place, for whatever reason, use your coaching voice to fight the *fear* that's driving the emotion before trying to fight the situation.

WITNESS YOUR INNER AND OUTER EXPERIENCE

This is another technique for those who struggle with self-nurturing. Witnessing is a technique associated with the principles of mindfulness. It is performed exactly as you think it might be: you observe—not just a little bit, but a lot—your experience as though you were in a strange science experiment doing formal research. Simply observe and describe your outer experience and then observe and describe your inner response to this experience. Try to truly *witness* your experience rather than finding ways to change it. Just observe and describe and observe and describe and then observe and describe some more. Observe with great curiosity everything that is happening around you, as well as in your body, your mind, your energy. Observe your deeper fear that is driving the negative response.

Radically witnessing an experience gives the mind something to focus on so that it doesn't start its "you need to, have to, got to, should" routine. After describing for a bit, you will still feel emotion, but you will not be swept up in it. And because you are not swept up, you are more likely to wisely and calmly respond to your situation rather than react to it impulsively. When you describe an experience long enough, you might find that you are able to lower the intensity of the emotion enough to engage some of the other fear-soothing techniques in this book. Or you might find, just as a watched cloud eventually dissipates, that a watched experience runs its course and naturally fades.

This technique can be particularly helpful for depression that is making you too foggy to think, or anger that has you too heated for any of the other techniques. Some people like to use the technique for food cravings as a way to observe an impulse to eat rather than compulsively act on it. Many of my clients find this to be one of the easier tools to turn toward, especially when an emotion is intense, and accessing nurturing just doesn't feel possible.

SHIFT YOUR CORE QUESTION

I personally use this technique a lot. In our culture, when we encounter a challenge, we have been trained to quickly and automatically ask ourselves the following question: "What do I do?" In fact, this question guides us all day long, often with the inclusion of the word *have* in it: "What do I *have* to do?" And when this question guides our minutes, our days, our weeks, what happens is that all our thoughts, emotions, and actions arise from and center around this question. We frantically do, do, do, or think about what we need to do, do, do, or feel guilty about what we should do and didn't do, and in the end, we just have a lot of do-do. (Ha! Did you see how that cleverly played out?)

But I want you to take a moment and recite the question, "What should I do?" in your mind. Feel the question in your body. Just notice for a moment how your body and energy subtly respond to it. How does the question make you feel?

For many of us, this question produces inner tension and unwittingly triggers a subtle stress response of fight, flight, or freeze. For example, if you tend toward anxiety, which as you know is a flight response, you likely feel tension and pressure, or some jittery energy when you ask, "What do I do?" If you tend more toward depression, which is a freeze response, you likely feel overwhelmed or hopeless. If you tend toward irritability, which is a fight response, perhaps you think about how others will get in the way of what you can do.

Now I'm going to have you ask yourself another question, and you don't have to think of a specific situation, just hold the question itself in your being and see how your body, mind, and energy responds to it. Here it is: ***Who do I want to be in this situation?***

Do you feel a change in your body and energy with this question? It's okay if you don't. You didn't do anything wrong. But for many of us, this question brings us pause. It slows us down rather than speeds us up. It shifts our perspective to our values and beliefs. It deepens us to a place of spirit.

And as a part of emotional health and living our best life possible, *this* is the question we need to be asking ourselves over and over and over again. "Who do I want to be?" The beauty of this, when we repeatedly practice answering this question, is that we very naturally also figure out the question of "What do I *do*?" but the answer comes from a place of spirit, rather than a place of fear.

As an example, one of my clients was going through a very difficult divorce. She and her soon-to-be ex-husband seemed unable to agree on even a single detail of how to manage their finances or their possessions, let alone how to co-parent their children.

One particular session, she was very distraught because she had just received a text from her husband saying he would no longer agree to the parenting schedule they had spent weeks trying to sort out. In tears and overwhelmed, she asked, "Heidi, what in the world do I *do*?" I assured my client that we would eventually answer that question but asked that we first spend just a little bit of time soothing her body and mind. She was asked to soften her breath, release the tension in her muscles, and shift her inner narration to a more nurturing and soothing tone. And when she was a bit more settled, I asked her, "Who do you want to be in this situation?" She responded that she wanted to be someone who is calm, strong, and steady. She wanted to stay easy and grounded under pressure.

As she said this, I saw her demeanor change. She was quiet for a moment and said, "I know what I need to do. I need to calmly and neutrally text my husband that he needs to communicate his wish with his lawyer, and then I will review his request with mine." When my client knew who she wanted to be—quiet, calm, solid—her next actions became more obvious to her.

The following are some other guiding questions that can dramatically shift our responses to stressful situations:

What have I done for this situation in the past? This question is often posed by counselors and therapists. Some life situations are brand-spanking new to us, in which case, the question "What have I done for this in the past?" might only be minimally useful. But most of our struggles are already familiar to us—an argument with our significant other is probably not a virgin experience. Being worried about our performance at work is probably not a shiny new sensation.

Reflecting on our past responses to struggles can be helpful in a few ways. First, we might jog our memory for something that actually worked in the past—that's the best-case scenario. Second, we might be reminded that we have survived similar struggles. This, in itself, can be reassuring even if it doesn't directly address our current situation. Third, we might be reminded of what didn't work in the past, so we don't just keep repeating the same tired responses.

Let me provide an example of a client for whom this simple technique had a big impact. Rosa had a rather difficult mother. She loved her mom and valued spending time with her, but this mom tended to talk nonstop and would interrupt Rosa before she could even complete a basic sentence. Rosa's fight response would kick in and she would find herself irritable, biting her cheeks and holding her breath.

When I asked her what she had tried for this situation in the past, she exclaimed, "That's the problem. I always respond in the exact same way and it doesn't work. I always bite my cheeks and scream in my head!" And then Rosa paused for second and said, "You know what? There was one time where I just broke down crying. I had had a difficult day at work and I was stopping by my mother's when I was both emotionally drained and physically spent, and when she started interrupting me, I just broke down. And for once my mother stopped, asked me what was wrong, and listened to me vent about my day."

Now this insight did not mean that Rosa realized she needed to cry every time she saw her mother. But it did show her that becoming soft and vulnerable was probably going to have a better shot at slowing down her mother than becoming physically hard and just tuning her out. She decided that a new approach would be to soften her breath and body and, with vulnerability, tell her mother she had some things to share that she'd really like her to hear. Even if this didn't work every time, it definitely improved her chances of getting her mother to listen.

What adverb do I want to apply? In our culture, when it comes to grammar, we have a strong focus on the nouns and verbs of our lives. We think a lot about the things we have, need, or want, and we talk a lot about what we do, need to do, or want to do. But there is a part of grammar, oft forgotten and little talked about, that has a huge impact on our lives, and that's the adverb. To refresh your memory, an adverb is a word or phrase that describes a verb.

As a psychologist, you begin to see that adverbs are extremely important from an emotional health perspective. At the end of the day, we all have the same verbs in our lives. Common verbs include: *work, exercise, sleep, cook, eat, socialize, take care of, love, worship* … the list goes on.

But what distinguishes us as humans are the adverbs that we apply to those verbs. Do you work frantically, or do you work gently? Do you exercise forcefully, or do you exercise lovingly? Do you eat shamefully, or do you eat with relish? Do you socialize anxiously, or do you socialize joyfully? Do you look in the mirror hatefully or with appreciation? Do you look at problems hopelessly or with curiosity? Do you rest wholeheartedly, or do you rest guiltily?

I could go on and on, but you get the idea. The verbs tell us about our outer state, but the adverbs we use reflect our *inner* state, and our inner state dictates the quality of our life.

Adverbs, in their most extreme form, show how certain verbs can spiral out of control. Someone who is an alcoholic drinks needily or recklessly. Someone who has an eating disorder eats hatefully. Someone who is a workaholic works obsessively. Someone who is an abuser in a relationship loves controllingly. (Yes, I know that's not a word, but I didn't want to ruin the rhythm.) Again, I could go on and on, but at the end of the day, show me a mental health issue and I'll show you someone using the wrong adverb.

So how do we shift this? By becoming conscious of the adverb we're using. My suggestion is, if you're a to-do list writer, spend some time make a coinciding "*how-to-do* list." Get groceries easily. Write email lightly.

Drop off kids deep-breathingly. (Yes, there's another made-up word, but you have to admit, it's sort of catchy.) If you're not a to-do list person, simply write "HOW am I doing what I'm doing?" on a piece of paper and stick it in your pocket for a few days so that every time you stumble upon it, you can ask yourself, for whatever it is you're doing in that moment, exactly how are you attending to it?

For giggles, go ahead and do this exercise *now*, right this very moment. How are you reading this book? Are you reading it intensely? Or are you reading it relaxedly? (Okay, I'm getting carried away now.) Are you dialoguing with the ideas in this book in a rigid way, or are you engaging in an open-minded way? Are you breathing shallowly or softly? Changing our adverbs from driven and hard ones to soothing and loving ones is an excellent way to help shift our emotional states.

What thought soothes me a little bit? This is a nice and simple core question technique that can be helpful when you're getting swept into negative thinking and you just don't have the energy or wherewithal to switch to a more positive mindset.

Instead just ask, "What thought soothes me a little bit?" The psyche can respond to this simple inquiry in an infinite number of ways. For me, the question brings up a different response every time. Sometimes I think about something as simple as what I'm going to eat for supper. Sometimes wise or helpful words come into my head. Sometimes I see random images of kittens. Sometimes I'm reminded to at least take a few deep breaths. "What thought soothes me a little bit?" is a great question to ask yourself several times throughout the day for a little mental reprieve.

FIND A CORE MANTRA

As a child, did you read *The Little Engine That Could*? If you haven't, spoiler alert ahead. In the book, the little "baby" train made it to the top of a very steep and scary hill by repeating the mantra, "I think I can. I think I can." When the going got tough, it didn't hinder the Little Engine That

Could. His innermost voice kept on with "I think I can, I think I can." In the end, it was the Little Engine's powerful phrase that allowed him to successfully tackle the nasty mountain.

The reality is, we are all Little Engines and we all have a core inner voice guiding us on our tracks. Unfortunately, for most of us, our core phrase is decidedly not "I think I can." Instead, it's something that comes from the mind and we've heard it already in this book several times: "I need to, I have to, I've got to, I should, I need to, I have to, I've got to, I should ..."

Or for some, the phrase might play out in the negative:

"I shouldn't have, I can't believe I, why didn't I ... "

And I think we all know at least one or two people with the following mantras:

"It's all about me. It's all about me."

"Like me, like me, like me, like me!"

"I can't. That won't work. I can't. That won't work."

The good news is, with mindfulness and practice, we can change the voice of our Little Engine. But first we need to decide what we would like our deepest inner voice to say. If you could have one phrase, at the core of your being, gently nudging you along, what would it be? Stop and truly take some time to contemplate your ideal core inner mantra. I'm going to offer a few suggestions based on what others have created:

"I've got this. I've got this. I've got this."

"Breathe in. Breathe out."

"Slow down and smile. Slow down and smile."

Mine is, "Light and easy." When partner Pete is telling me that he wouldn't mind a pair of moose antlers on the wall, I come back to my mantra of "light and easy." When my cat coughs up a hairball on my cream-colored carpet: "light and easy." And when a client points out that I have lunch leftovers in my teeth, I say, once again, "light and easy." This mantra may not take away my stress, but it guides me toward a wiser response to my stress.

GET NURTURING AND SOOTHING FROM OTHERS

Some fears are easily soothed on our own, but others require troop support. Asking for help with our fears can be a very effective way to soothe the mind. Women tend to naturally turn toward this technique when they confide their problems to their friends. Men, sadly, don't do this as much. They still experience great pressure to present as outwardly strong and impenetrable.

No matter who you are, you need to be selective when you tell others about the fears underneath your emotions. We all deserve friends and connections who are nurturing and supportive rather than judgmental and condemning, but not everyone has this luxury. If you don't have someone in your life who intuitively knows how to comfort and soothe, don't panic, you can learn to meet this need yourself over time (and when you do, you will likely attract more nurturing and supportive people into your life). Of course, you can also get better at it by using some of the fear-soothing techniques in this book.

And if you *are* someone who's blessed with wonderful friends/partners/family members, you should still be careful. Turning to them shouldn't be the *only* fear-soothing skill you cultivate. There's a fine line between getting healthy reassurance from others and being needy, and that line is whether you also incorporate several fear-softening techniques or whether getting help from others is your one-trick pony (by the way, I would love a one-trick pony just as much as a many-trick pony—they're so darn sweet).

GO DOWN THE RABBIT HOLE OF FEAR

I see many people intuitively use this tool all on their own. The Down the Rabbit Hole technique helps you to stop and dig into the fear or fears underneath your current negative emotion. It involves asking yourself, over and over again, "What am I afraid of right now, and why am I afraid of that?" Then, once you figure out the answer, you ask, "And why in the bejiminy am I afraid of that?" And when you have an answer to *that*, you ask, "Well, what the behoopdie am I afraid of that for?"

At the end of the day, when we honestly, truly, deeply examine our fears, often we realize that we actually *could* deal with them if we had to. Sometimes the fear just magically disappears altogether. Let me give you a common example. So many people feel stress at their jobs. And what's the fear driving the stress?

Generally, it's that if they don't keep up with their jobs, they will get fired. Duh, right? But why are we so afraid of getting fired? Because we would take a serious financial hit and we don't know how long it would be before we found another job. Why then are we afraid of pinching pennies and looking for another job? Because we fear we would go bankrupt and never find another job. OK, but why are we afraid of going bankrupt and not finding another job? Because it would be hard to recover from bankruptcy and not finding a job would be embarrassing. Whew, this is exhausting … Well then, why are we afraid of a tough financial recovery and embarrassment? Because we fear being uncomfortable and having people think badly of us. And why are we afraid of being uncomfortable and of what other people think? I dunno, we just are …

OK, that's enough of that, but let me tell you what starts to happen with this technique: First, at some point, you realize that your fear is ridiculous and not worth getting all squeaky at. Or you realize that even though it's not pleasant, you *could*, if you really had to, handle your worst fear. You could deal with getting fired and bankruptcy, if it came to that. You could handle it if other people judged you and thought you'd never get a job again (chances are they're too busy trying not to get fired themselves to think about you in the first place).

You wouldn't *like* tolerating these things, but deep down you know you could. Often our worst fears, when we make them conscious, are either 1) silly or 2) tolerable if we really truly think about it. *And even if our worst fears are very real, it is still helpful to get to the deepest level of fear so that we can more skillfully attend to it.*

DISTRACTION (AND WHEN TO USE IT)

Distraction is exactly as it sounds—finding something to focus on so that we don't think about our stress. Our culture sends us mixed messages about this technique. On the one hand, we have all heard that it's bad to deny our emotions, that we should feel our feelings, etc. On the other hand, we constantly tell people when they're feeling overwhelmed: "Don't worry about it. Just relax."

I worked with a client who lost her husband tragically and unexpectedly. A quiet person, she had friends and family, but saw them only occasionally. She and her husband had preferred being at home together. At his funeral, people were very supportive and told her to take time to heal and grieve. However, shortly after the funeral, she was barraged with well-meaning invitations for dinners, weekend getaways, walks, and happy hours. On the one hand, she was receiving the message that she should just take time to be sad. On the other, she was hearing that she should stay busy, think positive, and move forward right away. Both messages were coming from a loving place, but it was very confusing for the client to navigate.

In her case, distraction was not necessarily the best technique. But it's different for everyone. Let me see if I can offer a formula for when distraction is beneficial and when it is not. In my experience, it is most helpful when other mind-soothing approaches haven't worked and the fear underneath the negative emotion is truly a "wheel-spinning" fear.

This means that a part of you knows, no matter how much you think about something, you're not going to be able to soothe or solve it, and nothing will change about the situation. In this case, distraction is a perfectly healthy approach. For example, I use distraction when I am frustrated with another person and I know no matter how much I think about it, the person or the situation is not going to change. All of my frazzled thinking on the topic will do nothing more than fill the world with more negative energy.

When you know you cannot change something, distraction is a perfectly healthy way of managing your emotion. But remember: negative emotions are also trying to give us the power to make some sort of change to our circumstances, even if they are slightly misguided at times. Anxiety is trying to motivate us to get away from a problem. Depression is trying to get us to slow down. Anger is trying to empower us to take action. We do need to stop and listen to what our emotions want and crave—and then decide whether they have a valid point.

So if you feel angry, and you sense that staying with this anger will empower you to take action in a positive way, stay angry and don't distract! But if your anger is wheel-spinning anger, where the same thoughts are just circling and circling, but there isn't a gol' durn thing you can do about the situation, then by all means … *distract*. If your anxiety is motivating you to productively fix a problem, do not distract. But if your anxiety is about something that could happen in the future and there is nothing you can currently do to prevent it, go ahead and distract. If your depression is pushing you to simplify, rest and reflect, don't distract. But if your depression is a whirlpool of self-deprecating thoughts that aren't teaching you anything, distract.

Distraction is just what it sounds like: doing something different to take your mind off your stress. Pick up a book, turn on the TV, spend time with others, work, even eat and have a drink! But be smart about it. Read a fun book, not one you feel like you *should* read. Watch something light and uplifting, not something that brings your mood down further. Listen to music that reflects how you want to feel, not music that enhances your current emotion. Eat to balance your blood sugar and mindfully savor your drink; don't drown in junk food and booze.

Like some of the other emotion-management techniques in this book, make sure that distraction is not your instant go-to for all difficult emotions (many people are at risk of this). Distraction really should be a tool selected with awareness, not a mindless habit.

FIND WHAT YOU TRUST

I've said over and over again that negative emotions have a vulnerable underbelly (which is fear) that wants to be soothed (not solved). But what is the psychological antidote to fear? Most people guess courage, and this is true for managing outer-world challenges. If you're afraid to jump from the high dive, you need a burst of courage to take action. But what about when we can't do anything to change our outer world and we're just trying to stabilize our inner one? What counters fear then?

Trust. Trust is a little-talked-about psychological orientation, but it is arguably one of the most important tools available to us in mental health. Why is it such a big deal? Because trust melts fear. I'll say that again: Trust melts fear.

We are all naturally wired with a deep well of trust that shows up in many forms: trust in our ability to cope, learn, and grow. Trust in our resources and supports. Trust in our ability to heal. Trust in the greater universe. Trust in our meaning and purpose. Trust is one of the seminal ingredients of resilience. When we have the deep-rooted trust that we can handle anything, we feel a deep sense of comfort and well-being.

Fear is yin and trust is yang, and we're wired to experience both, but there's a slight problem. We don't have to lift a finger to access fear. Fear floods us all day long in various ways and levels of intensity. We don't have to think about or try to summon it. We get a steady supply of fear just waking up in the morning and being alive.

Trust, on the other hand, needs to be consciously accessed. It's pretty rare for trust to manifest all on its own. We have to stop and actively identify what we trust. Trust is a practice and a discipline.

So the technique here is this: When you experience a really tough emotion, identify the fear and then ask yourself over and over again: what do I trust that could melt this fear just a little bit? Then: what *else* do I trust that will help melt the fear? And what else? Only respond to fear with what you actually and truly trust, not what you kinda-sorta trust. And if you initially only trust negative things, or don't know what you trust, keep asking: what *else* do I trust that helps this fear a little bit? I promise you, because we are all wired the same, that you will eventually find something you trust that will help to soften or melt the fear, at least a little bit.

Let me give you a personal example. When I was working on my psychology degree, I was anxious all of the time. And when I analyzed the fears, I found that I had many. Fears were coming at me from all directions. I feared I would fail. I feared I wouldn't be good at this profession. I feared I had made a mistake going back to school. I feared I wouldn't get everything done. I feared I would never feel rested or happy again.

But when I really looked at my fear, I realized my biggest fear of all was about what other people were thinking of me. I was older when I started my degree, and it took me a wee bit of extra time to complete it (which is a sarcastic way of saying it took nine years), since I worked full-time and completed some parts of my schooling slower than the typical student. While everyone around me was seemingly successful, living in nice homes and taking family vacations, I was broke, alone, and lost in textbooks. I feared (a lot actually) that people thought I was a loser, that I was spinning my wheels and that I had no life. These fears were sometimes conscious, but often lurking just beneath the surface.

When I asked myself, "What do I trust?" the process was slow to start. My psyche would respond with something like, "I trust that this will be worth it someday." But if I kept asking the question, I found there was more to trust than I originally thought. I trusted that my life had its own purpose. I trusted that eventually I wouldn't be a student anymore. I trusted that others probably weren't even thinking about my life—at least not most of the time. I trusted that I was actually pretty darn loved by some.

All of these were mildly helpful, but then, suddenly, I thought of something else … something I trusted that dramatically softened the fear. In this case, the magic thought was: "I trust that it's human and normal to have to tolerate a little judgment from others." Now, I don't honestly understand why this particular thought softened my psyche above all of the others. But, for some strange reason, this trust smoothed out my emotions, allowed me to take a deep breath and keep plowing forward (for the record,

I think I could write an entire book on the psychological power of being able to tolerate judgment from others, but finish reading this book first …).

Let me provide a more serious example. In 2004, as some of you will recall, a tsunami of historical proportions devastated the coastlines of several countries along the Indian Ocean, killing well over 200,000 people, and displacing nearly two million. It was the day after Christmas, and the news was filled with horror stories of the people killed, sometimes entire families, in mere seconds.

As people tend to do, my friends and I talked about how we couldn't imagine experiencing a tsunami, or how a person who lost their entire family could ever possibly recover. With a shudder, we tried to picture ourselves in this situation. Most of us said that the pain would be unbearable, and we would likely live a zombie-like existence for our own remaining days.

However, one friend (I call her "Colorado Kate") gave a different response. Colorado Kate is a happily married mother of two. She is passionate about parenting and has one of the tightest-knit families I know. I thought for certain Colorado Kate, of all people, would say that if she lost her family in a natural disaster, her life would no longer be worth living. But Kate's response surprised me. She said, being the sole survivor of a tsunami would be the hardest thing she could ever imagine enduring, and she knew she would need a lot of time to feel angry and grieve for her family and disconnect from the world. But then, Kate said, she would eventually try to create an entirely new life, likely one that bore no resemblance to her first one, since that would be too painful. For example, maybe she would join the Peace Corps and dedicate her life to service.

We were aghast that Kate could talk about a life beyond her family— even hypothetically. But Kate was not being callous or cold. She simply had something special that the rest of us lacked. Even with the most awful and painful thing she could imagine, Kate trusted that life could be rebuilt. She had the deep-rooted trust that she could handle anything the world dealt her. Kate had true emotional resilience.

TALK WITH YOUR EXPECTATIONS

This is a mind-soothing technique that I like to use for frustration or anger. Anger, in any manifestation, is a tough emotion to soothe. Anger is our system trying to give us strength to change something, regardless of whether we can or not. In an effort to hang on to the invigorating sense of power and righteousness that anger gives us, our minds tend to repeat the same thoughts over and over in an effort to keep us ticked off. We don't want to soothe when we're pissed!

However, if you'll recall, all negative emotions have a vulnerable or fear-driven underbelly, and anger is no exception. Anger can stem from many sources, but one of the most common triggers underneath our fight response is *fear of an expectation not being met*. Now I realize anger doesn't *feel* like the fear of an expectation not being met. What anger feels like is a whole lot of swear words about to happen. But at the end of the day, all negative emotions are a form of fear or imbalance, and the fear under much of anger is that an expectation is being disregarded. We get angry when others do not meet our expectations, whether it be our coworkers, our partners, our children, our politicians, or just the general human population. We also get angry with ourselves when we fail to meet our own expectations.

Managing expectations is a particularly challenging area of emotional health, because our expectations always seem reasonable to us, and anger feels perfectly justified when you're in the throes of it. For this reason, we tend to hold on to our expectations (and our anger) quite rigidly. When we experience an expectation that's not being met, we harden rather than soften. We try to be strong rather than resilient. Our bodies tense. Our minds steel. Our energy becomes sharp and our words become incisive.

We very naturally want to *enforce* our expectations, not soothe them. And in a small percentage of cases it's important and right to enforce our expectations—namely when it comes to situations involving justice or safety.

For example, if you see someone being victimized and you have the expectation that this is wrong, I want you to rigidly hold on to the expectation and help the person being victimized! But in most cases, when others are not meeting our expectations, these expectations have nothing to do with justice or safety. And in most cases, when others are not meeting our expectations, there's not a jiminy-cricket thing we can do about it. When that's the case, we need to soothe.

Here's what I promise—you do not have to get rid of your expectations. Admittedly, sometimes our expectations are ridiculous (like the hotel guest I saw yelling at the front-desk staff because the birds outside her room window were too loud). Other times our expectations are tied to our deepest and most important human values. Either way, whether your expectations are absurd or justified, we need to learn when to enforce them and when to soothe them. And we need a way to navigate the reality that we will never ever ever ever *ever* live in a world where everyone else agrees to and adheres to our particular expectations. Ever.

So what do we do about this? We cultivate a healthy, dynamic, and flexible relationship with our expectations. We soften our grip on our expectations without relinquishing them completely. And the trick to this is to have a soothing conversation with your expectations. I know, this seems sorta strange, not to mention dopey. But me-oh-my can a person's quality of life alter significantly when they learn to soothe unmet expectations rather than become enraged by them.

Let's see if we can clarify this concept with some examples. I'll start with a personal one. I happen to be a very conservative driver and have been called "grandma" by more than one passenger. But my cautious nature does not prevent me from experiencing a rather unseemly and embarrassing case of road rage. My sudden driving tantrums are usually caused by the exact same thing—merging into highway traffic from an entrance ramp. Being a considerate driver, I do what is expected of a merging automobile. I politely turn on my blinker, accelerate, and begin to look for an opening on the highway (always checking my blind spot of course).

Sometimes, and this happens more often than I want to admit to you, the car directly behind me on the entrance ramp will swing into the next lane, hit the accelerator, and pull forward and take the spot that was supposed to be mine. This leaves me either driving into the shoulder or slamming on the brakes. If you want to see a Bambi-loving incense-burning psychologist throw a hissy-fit, just pull up behind me on an entrance ramp and cut off my opening. This scenario incites my fight response, and it takes every cell of my being not to charge my adorably tiny, but impressively strong Fiat directly into the rear end of your silly whatever-it-is car.

At some point, I realized that this particular frustration was something I needed to tend to. So over coffee one morning I had a conversation with myself. It started by finding the trigger for my driving anger, which wasn't hard to do. My trigger was the very fair and reasonable expectation that others drive with courtesy and consideration. The good news is, I do not need to change my expectation! And you don't need to change your expectations either. But I do need a more flexible relationship with this particular expectation, and I do this by having a loving chat with myself about it. And you need to have a loving chat with your expectations too. It looks something like this: "Heidi, it's fair to expect others to drive courteously. But we live in a world where our expectations are only met a small percentage of the time, and you need to breathe and manage the truth of this. And luckily, most people *do* drive politely. Only a small percentage of drivers are bumble-headed-ninny-dopes."

Soothing your expectations cannot often be done in the heat of the moment. For this technique, you might need to study the areas of your life where you are repeatedly becoming angry, examine the expectations that are not being met, and find the talk that soothes or softens your grip on those expectations a little bit. Then, the next time you are triggered, you will hopefully be quicker about finding a soothing thought in the heat of the moment. Now, when I am cut off on a merge, my process is automatic. I first get enraged and point my not-nice finger. Then I quickly say, "*Most* people don't drive like that," and I am able to recover much more quickly.

Let me give you another example. Sai found himself getting angry with his coworkers. He was an assiduous and conscientious employee at his company, and he did not feel he was in a work culture that valued the same. In fact, he often felt taken advantage of for his work ethic—being burdened with extra projects and hours while his coworkers nonchalantly left early for a happy hour. Sai had the expectation that others work as hard as he did. Sai came to me because his anger was eating him up and bleeding into his personal life.

First of all, Sai's anger was his fight response, and a fight response is always trying to give us the power to change something. However, Sai was helpless to use this power because he desperately needed this job to build his resume and support his family. That being said, we did help Sai more productively use some of his anger by outlining a reasonable time line for updating his resume and exploring other job options.

We also talked about ways he could assertively communicate his experience to his supervisor. Taking small actions helped Sai feel empowered and more optimistic. But as with most situations that produce anger, Sai couldn't immediately change his circumstances. And because Sai was incredibly diligent, the reality was that even with a new job he might find himself in the exact same situation. This means we needed a Plan B, which was to cultivate resilience.

So, Sai and I studied his expectation and looked for a softer way to dialogue with it. Sai didn't need to change his work ethic, nor did he need to lower his expectations of others. But he did need to have a more balanced internal dialogue around his expectation. Sai's reflexive response any time the topic of work expectations came up was, "My coworkers are all lazy jerks!" But as we explored his expectation, Sai was able to soften a bit. He was able to say things like, "I do value hard work, but I need to breathe around the reality that not everyone shares this value. And someday, this value might really pay off for me if I'm patient. In the meantime, I can continue to live my values and feel proud of myself for doing so."

With time and practice, Sai was able to incorporate resilient self-talk in the heat of triggered moments. On really good days, he was even able to bolster himself with, "I love my work values. I wish others could feel how good hard work feels." Did softer dialogue around his expectation completely vanquish his anger? No. The trigger continued to arise, but it was much more easily managed. Did softer dialogue with his expectation change his expectation of others? Nope—but he was able to feel more sympathy for them rather than resentment. And he was also able to identify that not all of his coworkers were as lackadaisical as he initially thought. Developing a soft dialogue with his expectation made him more resilient, and being more resilient made life more bearable.

Dialoguing with, and softening, our relationship to our expectations is a tough concept for most of us. We have been raised in a culture that says we should fight, push, strive to get our way. Yes—sometimes! When every cell of your being tells you to fight, push, and strive to enforce your expectations because you really believe it will help, go for it. But for *most* situations, you can kick and spit all you want, but all you'll end up with is sore toes and soggy clothes.

When you can't change something, become resilient in the face of it. And to become resilient, soothe your expectations.

Let's explore another common example. Many people feel anger when they watch the news. They have the expectation that we live in a safe and fair world, and watching the news shows us the gazillion ways we humans are failing to meet these expectations. Not for one hot second do I want you to give up your expectations of a safe and fair world. And when you can directly contribute to a safe and fair world, for the love of all things Dolly Parton please take action and do so!

But even when you can contribute to a fair and safe world, your expectation that the world be 100% safe and 100% fair will never be met. What then? Soothe your expectations by talking to them. "I will continue to strive toward a safe and fair world, and I will try to believe that we're very slowly moving toward more safety and fairness in time. But I also need to breathe, stay soothed, and conserve strength when I can't do anything."

See how that works? This technique will not allow you to get your way, nor will it make you euphoric and happy. But it will take the edge out of your fight response in situations you can't fight. It will boost your general resilience.

SUMMARY TIME

Mind-soothing techniques are all variations of one basic concept: soothing the fears at the root of negative emotions. Find the fear and baby it a little. Find the fear and sing about it. Find the fear and courageously challenge it. Find the fear and neutralize it with description, soft attention, curiosity. Find the fear and decide the type of person you want to be in response to the fear. If the fear is a wheel-spinning fear that all the thinking in the world won't help, distract from the fear. Find the fear and figure out what you trust that softens the fear. And if that doesn't work, find some thoughts or dialogue, any thoughts or dialogue, which *do* provide a little relief.

CHAPTER 9

HOW DO WE INVOLVE SPIRIT
IN OUR EMOTIONAL HEALTH?

Ahh, we've arrived at my favorite part of the mind-body-spirit trio. SPIRIT. I've already emphasized that everyone has to come to their own definition of *spirit*. The way that you personally explain the feeling of being alive, creative, connected, value-driven, loving, vital, and present in the world—that's spirit.

Here's the good news. Everything we talked about in the body section of this book is designed to soften tension in the body in order to create room for the spirit. And everything we talked about in the mind section of this book is designed to soften tension in the mind in order to create room for the spirit.

Our spirits want us to fulfill our nature and our potential. Our spirits also want us to express our deeper values, not our mind-derived beliefs of "need to, have to, got to, should." There are reasons, however, that we don't live from a place of spirit all the time. First, we tend to block the spirit by holding chronic and habitual tension in the body. Second, we tend to block the spirit by holding chronic and habitual tension in the mind.

But living from a place of spirit can be challenging in other ways. Sometimes what our spirits want doesn't align with what our family and friends think is best for us, or what our culture or religion tells us, or what our mind thinks we need-to-have-to-got-to-should-do. Living from a place of spirit might require you to rebel against certain aspects of your upbringing or your world. Not always, but sometimes. And living from a place of spirit takes courage. For example, a person who identifies as transgender may have mind talk that says, "I *need* to be the sex I was born. I *have* to act 'normal.' I've *got* to do what my parents want for me. I *should* be happy as I am." But his spirit says, "I am fundamentally in the wrong body for me."

To boot, living from a place of spirit can be perceived as self-centered. "If I do what my spirit really truly wants, it would be selfish and hurtful to others." It is my belief that we desperately need to redefine what is and isn't self-centered. In fact, I offer up a second term: *spirit-centered. Self-centered is any decision made for ego, image, power, shallow pleasure, or material gain. Spirit-centered is any decision made for the health of one's spirit.* Let me provide a common example. I live in the Midwest, where people often live close to their extended family. It's easy, when you have aunts, uncles, nieces, nephews, as well as dozens of cousins, to have the calendar quickly filled with school plays, potlucks, birthday parties, and holiday events.

In my counseling practice, I often hear clients complain that they desperately crave more restorative time *at home*. When they think of going to this wedding shower or that family barbecue, they feel something constrict deep within. I will argue that this is their spirit trying to express its needs for a simpler schedule. Alas, they feel obligated to attend the endless stream of social events because they don't want to hurt someone's feelings, be viewed as rude, or make others mad. Not attending would be, in their minds, "selfish." This seems especially true for women.

In my view, staying home is spirit-centered. Staying home allows the spirit to expand and soften and restore. Staying home is honoring one's deeper nature. At another time, one's spirit might crave the connection of family and say yes to the event at hand, but sometimes the spirit needs to stay home. Now, if you are staying home for ego, image, power, shallow pleasure, or material gain, *then* you are being selfish. Spirit-centered is honoring our deeper energy and going to the events that make us feel warm inside, and assertively putting up boundaries when our calendars feel too full.

I believe we need to accept the universal truth that we cannot get through this life without disappointing, letting down, or even hurting the feelings of others. It's simply not possible, even if we would like it to be. And who really wants to arrive at the end of their life and say, "I lived it politely and was never a bother to anyone!" My job as a therapist is to help my clients find the assertiveness and the language that will help them meet the needs of their spirit.

Again, self-centered is when something is for one's ego, image, power, shallow pleasure, or material gain. Spirit-centered is when we make decisions that expand and lighten our very cores. As men and women both, we need to learn to 1) make more spirit-centered decisions and 2) be more tolerant of others doing the same thing. It is my personal belief that if people truly made spirit-centered choices, even if those choices initially inconvenienced others, the world would fall into alignment over the big picture and everyone would benefit.

BUT WHAT DO SPIRITS NEED?

The overarching goal thus far in this book has been to remove tension from the body and the mind so that we can ignite the spirit. But what happens if we soothe the body and soothe the mind and we still don't feel vitality or love? What if we get to the level of the spirit and it doesn't feel all that spirited? Just as the body can be habitually tense or ill and the mind can be habitually rigid or fearful, the spirit can feel habitually burdened or constricted. Sometimes our spirits need a little bit of dusting off and waking up just like our bodies and minds.

Before I explain how to vitalize the spirit, I'm going to give you an exercise that I think is helpful for understanding your own spirit. I strongly suggest that you take a moment to complete this exercise before reading on. Now, if you're like me and often skip the exercises in books, thinking, "I'll do it later," make an exception for this one. It will take less than five minutes and can provide some interesting insight that will be used later in this chapter. I promise it's easy and interesting to do.

The exercise is pretty simple—I want you, without overthinking it, to complete the following sentences. Your responses can be, and likely naturally will be, short. Don't worry about whether what you write is negative, positive, smart, dumb, right, or wrong. Just see what flows off the tongue and put that down. Here are the sentences:

Work is …

My work …

Family is …

My family is …

Health is …

My health is …

Marriage or partnership or singleness is (pick the one that best applies) …

My marriage or my partnership or my singleness is …

Time is …

My time is …

Money is …

My money is …

The future is …

My future is …

Life is …

My life is …

Suffering is …

My suffering is …

People are …

The world is …

Rest is …

I am …

There, you did it! Give yourself a deep, rejuvenating breath and some nurturing self-talk while I give you some context for what we just did. Get your highlighter ready for this next part, because I'm about to tell you everything I know as a psychologist. Everything. Save yourself nine years of training and a dissertation. Read the next several paragraphs, and you and I will be on the same page. Here goes. Here's a basic theory about how the psyche works.

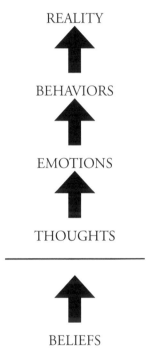

REALITY

BEHAVIORS

EMOTIONS

THOUGHTS

BELIEFS

This chart outlines the layers of our general human experience. Let's start at the top. We can all agree, I hope, that we are navigating a phenomenon called *reality*. And there are some things about reality that we can control and many things that we can't control. One thing that we can mostly (emphasis on mostly) control are our *behaviors*, which are all of our actions and day-to-day choices. We've all heard the phrase, "make good choices," and we learn from an early age that our behaviors are extremely important for shaping our realities.

But what drives our behaviors? Different people will give you different ideas, but in psychology, we believe *emotions* drive behaviors. Think about it. Everything you do is an attempt to achieve a positive emotion or get away from a negative emotion. You might say you are going to work to earn a paycheck, but scratch below the surface and you are going to work to get a paycheck because it feels better emotionally to provide for your family than to not be able to pay the bills. Or you might stay in a relationship that has grown stagnant because this decision produces easier emotions than the guilt that would be felt by leaving. Our behaviors are driven by a search for positive emotions and an avoidance of negative ones.

Okay, but what drives emotions? If you go to the self-help section of the bookstore, you will read that *thoughts* shape emotions. Think positive thoughts and you will experience positive emotions (which will lead to positive behaviors which will shape a more positive reality). Think negative thoughts and you will experience negative emotions (which will lead to negative behaviors which will shape a more negative reality).

There is a certain amount of truth in this, but have you ever tried to think positively about something and then actually ended up feeling worse—in part because you now feel like a failure at positive thinking? Positive thinking is a positive experience *when the positive thoughts are genuine.* But often, when we try to force ourselves to think positive, we say something that we don't actually believe. Then we feel even worse because our positive thinking isn't working, and we wonder what's wrong with us that we're so darn negative. So yes, thoughts do impact emotions, and we can alter emotions with the attitude behind our thoughts, but we can't lie to ourselves to change our emotions. So if positive thinking hasn't worked for you in the past, don't feel like a loser.

Okay, so what influences thoughts? Here's where we get to some juicy stuff. *Beliefs* influence our thoughts. *Beliefs are our ideas about how the world works and our value in that world.* I haven't repeated myself in a while, so allow me a little drama here. Beliefs are our ideas about how the world works and our value in that world.

It can be a little bit tricky to distinguish between beliefs and thoughts since they're both formed with language. Beliefs are different than thoughts in that they are not a part of day-to-day mind chatter—that's the thoughts. When you have thoughts about work, you're thinking about what you need to get done that day, problems that need to be solved, stressors that need to be dealt with. But your beliefs about work are not a part of your conscious dialogue. Some people believe hard work is the foundation of a good life. Some people believe that we should do the bare minimum at work and save our energy for other things. Some people believe that work is something we simply have to tolerate. Other people believe that work is where we express our passion and values. And it is your beliefs about work that are the foundation for all of your thoughts about work, which then lead to several of your emotions about work, which influence your work behaviors, which in turn cocreate your reality. Get it?

Let's try another example. Have you ever known someone who thinks that *all* people are selfish and untrustworthy? Many of us have. And it's astonishing to me how beliefs that everyone is out to get you lead to thoughts about how terrible people are, which lead to emotions about people that are sour and dour, which lead to dour and sour behaviors that—you see where this is going—lead to a reality where loving and trustworthy people don't want to be around you, and the only ones who can stand your company are selfish and untrustworthy.

Conversely, I have met individuals who truly, deeply, wholeheartedly believe that all people are wonderful, and I'll be darned if I don't see total jerks turn into purring sweethearts the moment they're around someone who truly believes in humankind. Think of Mother Teresa. She believed deeply in the value of every human and, as a result, I highly doubt anyone ever tried to give her a noogie or stick a finger in her cupcake frosting for fun. (I believe some people can be nincompoops, so that's probably why I've had numerous noogies and fingerprinted cupcakes in my lifetime …)

Now I'm not saying that our beliefs create every single aspect of our reality. There's a lot of reality happening at once, and my belief is that we only influence a part of that reality. But the part of reality that we *do* affect is influenced by our deepest beliefs about how the world works and our value in it. Here's another way to put all of this. Our *reality* is the sum total of our *circumstances*. Our *behaviors* are enacted with our *bodies*. Our *thoughts* are the language of the *mind*. Our *beliefs* are the language of the *spirit*. Our emotions come from all four of these realms: circumstances, body, mind, and spirit. But ...

> *It is by making changes at the level of the spirit—by directly engaging and challenging beliefs— that we can really pack a wallop on reality.*

I promise I'm going to discuss how we access and alter our beliefs. But let me first explain where our beliefs come from. Perhaps you can guess— it's your childhood. Depending on who you listen to, our beliefs about the world and our worth are pretty well formed by the age of 12. We learn these beliefs from our experiences, our families, our neighborhoods, our peers, our schools, our religions, our culture, etc. Before we even get all our adult teeth, we have a belief about whether we are good or bad, wanted or unwanted, have potential or don't, are likeable or not.

Then, as we age, we start applying those beliefs to our thoughts, emotions, and behaviors, which then creates our reality, which then reinforces our beliefs, which creates our thoughts, emotions, and behaviors, which then creates our reality, which then reinforces our beliefs, which reinforces our reality, which reinforces our behaviors, which ...

Are you seeing how this works? While conscious thoughts play a role in our life, it is really our subconscious beliefs that form the roots of our thoughts, emotions, behaviors, and subsequent circumstances. Beliefs are a key ingredient of reality.

HOW TO CHANGE OUR BELIEFS

Here's the good news. Beliefs can evolve and change during the course of our lives. Even though we're helpless to the beliefs we are exposed to as children, we can shape and evolve our beliefs as adults.

How?

Several ways, the first one being newness—new experiences, new people, new influences, new challenges, and new learning can deeply change and shift us. If you need an inner makeover, figure out a million new things you can do. Talk to people you wouldn't normally talk to. Explore places you've never explored. Take a class. Take a risk! Dress differently. Read a book in a different genre. Try a different approach to a problem. We never get to know beforehand how a new experience will impact the way we see the world. Sometimes even small risks are life altering.

Now to be fair, some new experiences can be negative and change our core beliefs for the worse. But I'm going to argue that we should never give up trying new things because the gains will likely outweigh the losses.

I'll never forget, in my early 30s, sitting next to an older man on a city bus. He was weathered and tattooed, wore filthy boots, and had clothes that had clearly seen physical labor. He smelled a little bit like onions and tar. His facial expression suggested that he did not want company. In my head, I built a picture of this man going home and polishing his machete collection. I hid in my book and tried not to breathe in an effort not to anger this dragon of a man.

Alas, he recognized the title of my book and, in a voice surprisingly like velvet, asked me if I had read any other books by this particular author. Because he had read them all! Turns out, we had a rather interesting discussion about strong female writers. This man was a laborer by day and a book/cigar aficionado by night.

I know we've all had experiences where we're reminded of the cliché: "Don't judge a book by its cover." My interaction with "dragon man" stirred up some beliefs in me that hadn't been present for a while—the belief that people are full of surprises and the belief that all humans have something sparkly and shiny inside them if you polish 'em just right. Though we only chatted for 15 minutes, if that, I spent the rest of the evening feeling lighter about the world and humankind.

If you just don't have the energy to try new things and talk to new people, there are other ways to access and alter core beliefs. Meditation is a potent one. Meditation, as we have already discussed, is the focused practice of softening the breath, quieting the mind, and accessing the spirit.

When we quiet our minds a wee bit we make room for our deeper beliefs about the world and ourselves to emerge. And when this happens, wise thoughts, new perspectives, solutions to problems, creative ideas, and deeper insights will sometimes (not always) effervesce to the surface without you lifting a pinky. Meditation can help us detach from the tiresome wheel-spinning mind and tune into our deeper values and beliefs. Meditation can also awaken shiny and new beliefs of the spirit that have been dormant or weren't present before.

My go-to meditation practice is yoga. Now, to be fair, not every yoga class brings me to a deep inner state of wisdom and enlightenment. Usually, I simply feel a general sense of pleasantness after a class.

But sometimes, and it's never predictable when, my spirit is awakened in a way that is euphoric. On these occasions, I will feel benevolent and lovey-dovey toward others. I will sense that my life has a purpose and that I'm on my right path. I will see that every human is part of the same quantum fabric. And I have to resist the urge to frolic down the sidewalk and giddily pinch people on the bum.

Yoga, or any meditation practice, has the power to summon powerful beliefs about the world and our place in that world. These heavenly and thrilling beliefs get lost in the hecticness of our 21st century demands, but when they are dusted off through meditation, our thoughts, emotions, behaviors, and reality all get a contact buzz.

In addition to new experiences and meditation, beliefs can be actively examined and challenged by a good mental health therapist. And if a therapist isn't available, beliefs can be consciously contemplated through reflection, discussion, and journaling. All you need to do is ask yourself, or have someone else ask you: What's something you believe about the world? And why do you believe that? And what's something you believe about yourself? And why do you believe that?

Repeat these questions over and over every day for the rest of your life. When you examine your beliefs head-on, you have the opportunity to challenge the ones that don't suit you and expand and enrichen the ones that do. And the more you live from your expanded and enriched beliefs about the world and your value in that world, the more you will see your thoughts, your emotions, your behaviors, and your reality expand and enrichen as well.

And finally, new beliefs can be ignited by the beliefs of others. When we read an inspiring book or hear an inspiring story or study an inspiring leader, our deepest beliefs about the world and our value can be shifted.

There is an entire field of study called transformational leadership. This approach to management and business focuses on galvanizing action rather than slave-driving it. And some of our history's greatest leaders were those who had the ability to stir the spirits of others. They incited those around them.

And think of how you feel after just the right book, your favorite song, or an edge-of-the-seat performance—*alive*. Any time we feel inspired, we are in a state of awakened or energized spirit. Inspiration is when we inwardly shift to a more vibrant spiritual belief about the world and our value in that world.

So how do beliefs fit into our *soothe* formula? When we are experiencing a challenging situation, we tend to give attention to our most negative beliefs about that situation, which then charge up through our thoughts, emotions, behaviors, and reality. And while we can't just get rid of negative beliefs— they are, after all, beliefs—we can look deep within ourselves and ask, *"Is there anything else I believe about this situation that gives me a bit more strength and resilience?" "Do I have any beliefs, that I actually believe, that help me?" "What is the lightest and most energizing belief I can access right now?"* We can then try to use that lighter belief to fuel our thoughts and emotions and behaviors and reality.

It is very important to note that we cannot use false beliefs. I would love to believe that life is easy and magical, that I always know what to say or do, and that I look amazing in skinny jeans, but I don't believe that. I believe that life is full of challenges and obstacles and that I am awkward much of the time, and that my butt is better off in yoga pants. Those beliefs feel like facts to me.

But if I dig deep, I can find *other* beliefs about life—that I actually believe but that have gotten a little lost in the shuffle—that can become a part of my reality-making. For example, while I believe life is full of obstacles, I also believe it's full of learning and growth. And though I can really put my foot in my mouth sometimes, I also believe I'm an insightful person who has a purpose in this world. And though I don't believe skinny jeans are for me, I do believe I embody my own unique beauty. But some days I lose track of these more vital beliefs, and I don't get the energy they provide to make my days lighter.

Again, it is important to distinguish between thoughts and beliefs, which can be challenging. Thoughts happen naturally in our head all day long. Beliefs are just below the surface of our awareness. We need to stop and put our beliefs into words because they are not an active part of our daily inner dialogue. Changing our thoughts isn't always all that helpful. We sometimes need to dig deeper, to the level of beliefs, to truly have an impact on our reality.

EXAMPLES OF BELIEF-SHIFTING

To summarize this whole darn book so far: when we are having challenging emotional experiences and there is nothing we can do to change our circumstances, we need to: 1) soothe the tension in our body, 2) soothe the fear in our minds, 3) vitalize our spirits by looking deeply inward and accessing our *best beliefs* about a situation. And I should warn you that sometimes our best beliefs aren't really all that positive. But if we start by finding the best beliefs available to us and practicing them consciously, we might find that beliefs slowly shift on their own over time.

Let me give you an example. My client (I'll call her Eve) was very depressed about not being in a romantic relationship. She had been single for a very long time, and the few liaisons she did have were abusive and dysfunctional in nature. Eve and I were working on a variety of issues, but when we explored her deepest beliefs around relationships, it was this: Men are violent and not to be trusted, and good relationships happen to a different type of woman than her. When Eve was asked if she believed she would ever find a relationship, she expressed a very assertive no. She did not believe there would be a rewarding relationship in her future. She didn't believe that this was how the world worked or what her value as a human warranted.

The problem with beliefs is that they feel like facts to us, they don't feel like beliefs. And just like we can't fake positive thoughts, we can't just pretend to believe better beliefs. I couldn't simply advise Eve to start believing in her worth or in the possibility of a healthy relationship for herself.

But we did start searching for lighter and brighter beliefs to challenge Eve's current negative ones. And, after lots of probing and discussion, Eve decided that the best belief about relationships that she could access was the following: "I could be wrong about my belief about relationships." That's it. That's the most positive belief we could summon that Eve truly believed. So I had Eve write that belief down and read it every day.

At first this admittedly did nothing for Eve, but she was diligent. And after several weeks, Eve started to observe a subtle shift. She began to notice that not *all* men seemed violent and abusive. And she also started noticing that many different types of women were in relationships, not just pretty and extroverted women, like she believed originally.

So I asked Eve if she could think of a belief that was even more vitalizing than "I could be wrong about my belief about relationships," and she decided upon this: "I believe a relationship without abuse might be possible for me." Now this is not a glowing, fairy-tale belief about love, but it is certainly lighter than Eve's original belief that all men are abusive.

So Eve wrote this belief down and read it every day. And again, nothing dramatic happened right away. But, over time she started to observe something new. She realized that she was looking men directly in the eyes and even engaging in small talk now and again. She also noticed an unexpected random thought at work of, "I'm not *that* different from other women." This was a new, and still fragile, belief that hadn't existed before, so we had Eve write this belief down and read it every day.

I'm afraid I am not going to give you a Hollywood ending to this story. The reality is, Eve stopped therapy and I do not know if she continued to improve her beliefs and, in tandem, her reality, over time. But I wanted to provide a realistic example of how a regular person can be walking around with some seriously heavy beliefs about how the world works (all men are violent and abusive) and her value in it (she is different from others and not worthy of a relationship). These beliefs could not be magically changed overnight.

However, as Eve accessed her most positive beliefs (which weren't all that positive) two things happened: She started observing the world a teensy, tiny bit differently, and her beliefs started to shift ever so slightly. And when she started to practice her new, more vital beliefs (I could be wrong about relationships and my value), this created space for even lighter beliefs (a relationship might be possible, and I might not be that different from others). Although these shifts were subtle, they had a compounding impact on Eve's emotional health. She started presenting as lighter. She smiled more and made more eye contact. And though she usually dressed all in black, she unexpectedly bought herself a yellow shirt for no reason that she could explain!

As an aside, do you see how Eve's beliefs were different from her thoughts? Eve wasn't actively thinking, "Go to work, send that email, men are violent and abusive, I am not worthy, I wonder what I should have for lunch today." Her beliefs were deeper undercurrents—assumptions that she didn't even know were influencing her. And these deeper assumptions can't just automatically be made cheery and positive. But in a tough situation, when we look deeply, we can often find a belief, something that we actually believe, that has a bit more energy behind it than whatever belief we are currently living from. And when we bring *that* better but believable belief to the forefront of our awareness, other levels of life start to subtly shift.

Let me give you another favorite example. My client (I'll call him Roger) was a 40-something male with a very demanding and argument-filled family. There was always some sort of drama between at least two family members, and spending time with family was usually a chaotic and draining experience. At the same time, Roger's family spent a lot of time together, and in their own way, were fiercely loyal to each other.

When we originally explored Roger's driving beliefs around family it was, "My family is bat-poop crazy" (for the record, he did not use the word bat *poop*). He had good reasons for this being his go-to belief. His family was admittedly a bit on the animal-dung crazy side of things. But I had Roger dig deep into his repository of beliefs, and he found that the lightest belief he could muster was, "My family is crazy most of the time, but not every single second."

Roger wrote this down and read it once a day. And it didn't take long for him to notice something. He reported that when he really looked at it, his family had just as many sane moments as bat-poop crazy ones. In fact, he started to see that the crazy moments really took up only a fraction of his time with family.

So Roger decided to play with a new belief. This time he chose, "I can breathe and be quiet during my family's craziness." Now this might not seem like an amazingly light and jovial belief about family, but for Roger this belief gave him more energy than most of his beliefs about family. So Roger practiced this belief for quite some time by reading it once a day. Sometimes he was successful in remembering to quiet and breathe during family dramas, sometimes he wasn't. But over time he found that he was not completely drained by family in the way he had once been.

Interestingly, Roger and I started talking about other areas of life, and the topic of family came up less and less. And when I brought this up, Roger shared that he had arrived at the belief that worked for him, and I'll never forget how he worded this: he said, "Family is crazy love." When Roger's family was immersed in their predictable imbroglios, he found himself breathing and observing from afar. And during these times, he found himself feeling an odd sense of humor and love. His belief of, "Family is crazy love," didn't change his family. They remained bat-poop crazy. But Roger's new belief allowed him to navigate his family from his highest self. From a place of spirit.

When you are in a tough emotional place, ask yourself: What do I believe about this situation? Then ask yourself, again and again and again: What else do I believe that is a little bit lighter? What else do I believe that gives me a little more energy or resilience? What else do I believe that makes me feel a wee bit better? Then write these beliefs down and practice them again and again. Beliefs take time to shift and energize, but the more work we do in this deep layer of our psyche, the more likely we will see concrete shifts in our reality.

GO BACK TO THE EXERCISE

Okay, let's go back to the core-belief exercise that I know you so diligently completed at the beginning of this chapter. Look at what beliefs rolled off the tongue. Where were they effortlessly positive? Where were they neutral? Where were they heavier and more negative?

To be fair, we have multiple and contradictory beliefs about all the topics outlined in that exercise, and on different days, you would likely provide different responses to the prompts. Some days, "Life is beautiful." Some days, "Life is hard." But over time, if we were to conduct this exercise every day, I'm guessing you would start to see that some topic areas consistently skew negative. These are the areas worth working on over time.

Go down the list and find your most negative beliefs. Then take some time to find the most vitalizing belief (*that you actually believe*) that you would like to practice instead. It doesn't have to be full of pixie dust and singing rainbows to be an effective belief. It just has to be 1) believable to you and 2) have more energy than your usual "go-to" beliefs on this topic. Then, write down your updated beliefs and place them somewhere where you will read them once a day. That's it. That's all you do. And when your updated list starts to lose its energy, or when you start to notice that you can access even *lighter* beliefs about a particular area, write those new beliefs down. Wash, rinse, repeat.

For the record, this is a lifelong exercise. It usually does not produce instant results (although on rare occasions it does!). I, myself, go through phases with this exercise. I tend to be committed to it in the spring, and then I get too busy in the summer to think about my beliefs. Then I'm remotivated in the fall. In the winter, Hulu® binges and snow shoveling take priority. Be kind with yourself if this doesn't become a disciplined and regular habit for you. Do it when you remember and have energy, and trust that any time we examine and refresh our deepest beliefs about the world and our value in it, we are doing something delicious for our spirits.

A SPECIAL NOTE ABOUT
YOUR BELIEFS ABOUT SUFFERING

Put on your scuba gear because we're going to dive deep here. There is one particular set of beliefs that I deeply encourage everybody to consciously examine—your beliefs about the nature and purpose of human suffering. I warned you—this gets heavy. As a therapist, I find that clients who have a conscious awareness of their beliefs about suffering—both their own suffering and the suffering of others—handle difficulty far better than those who don't. Let me explain …

Perhaps the most humbling privilege I have as a psychologist is connecting with the inner worlds of many different people from many walks of life. And the longer I'm in this profession, the more I see that although we are all having unique life experiences and different life challenges, we are all experiencing some form of suffering. Each and every one of us.

Some manifestations of suffering are more intense than others. Some suffering is physical. Much of suffering is mental. Some suffering is traumatic and life altering. Some suffering is minor. Some suffering is experienced as a constant undercurrent of difficulty. Some suffering is caused by others. Some suffering we create with our negative thinking and limiting beliefs. Some suffering is institutional and applies to entire groups of people. But we will all experience suffering in this life. And this has been true since the dawn of human existence and will likely remain true until its conclusion.

Alas, when we are in the middle of our own problems, we forget that the struggles we're having are *human* ones, and we assume they're due to something we're doing wrong in our lives. And then we get mad at ourselves, or mad at our God, or mad at other people. When we are in the throes of our own difficulties, we bemoan, "Why me??? What am I doing wrong???"

Let's take a relationship breakup as an example. This is something most people will experience—multiple times, even. But when someone is actually in the throes of a breakup, the self-talk becomes, "What is wrong with me? How could I have failed in this way? Am I being punished for some reason? How come *everyone else* has a perfect relationship? Why, why, why me? What am I doing WRONG?"

Dig deep. What do *you* believe about the purpose of suffering? Some religions say suffering happens when we do bad things, but I think every 21st century person knows that this doesn't match up with reality. Suffering happens to *everyone*, regardless of whether they're Mother Teresa or Joe Schmo. In your belief system, does the inescapable reality of suffering have a purpose? Do you have a conscious set of beliefs about how you should relate to your own suffering, as well as the suffering of others?

I implore this exploration for my religious friends, agnostic friends, and atheist friends alike. Even if you believe the cosmos is random, what are your beliefs about the nature of suffering and how we should attend to the universality of it? The next time you experience suffering (there's probably some suffering you can identify right this very moment), shift your core response from "Why me?" to "What am I going to do with this human experience?"

I personally believe that our own suffering makes us more compassionate. I believe our personal struggles are designed to help us learn and grow, and I believe the suffering of others gives us much needed perspective and reminds us of the important things in life. And I believe that stepping in and helping with the suffering of others is part of the purpose of our existence. I don't like that suffering exists, and don't get me started on how much I hate that trauma exists, and if you really want me to rant, let me tell you how much I hate that institutionalized suffering still runs rampant in the form of racism, sexism, homophobia, etc.

But when I'm in the middle of my own suffering, and when I see the suffering of others, I find it softens a little (and sometimes a lot) when I access my core belief that suffering cultivates compassion, drives me to help others, and perhaps has a larger universal purpose.

You don't have to share my beliefs about suffering. Nor does having a belief about the purpose of suffering mean we should become complacent about suffering—we need to actively challenge and fight our own suffering, the suffering of others, the suffering of entire groups, and the suffering of the planet. But at the end of the day, do you have a way of making sense of the fact that suffering happens to everyone, in different forms, throughout their lives? Does suffering have a purpose in your view? What do you believe we as humans need to do in the face of our own suffering? What do you believe our response should be to the suffering of others?

Finding our own philosophy of what we're supposed to do with the reality of suffering can make us more resilient, as well as provide us with a clearer perspective about how to manage life's challenges. When we are not lost in the self-talk of "Why me and what am I doing wrong???" we can shift to more helpful dialogue such as, "How do I stay resilient during my own suffering? How do I help the suffering of others?"

A BRIEF WORD ON DISCRIMINATION

The longer I'm in this field, the more I see that none of us escapes suffering. But one of the most insidious forms of suffering I see is institutionalized suffering: racism, homophobia, sexism, classism, anti-Semitism, discrimination against class, age, weight, etc. Any sort of suffering where a group of people is dismissed in a societal way is discrimination, and unfortunately, this form of suffering is one of the most challenging for me as a counselor to soothe.

Discrimination is the chronic and habitual societal onslaught of the message, "You are, at your very core being, less than others no matter what you say or do." Discrimination and institutionalized suffering are basically the world telling you that you are not good enough, not wanted, and don't belong. It's sometimes overt and said pretty much exactly just like that, but it's usually much more subversive. It's hidden in our assumptions, our language, our media images, our policies. It is unrelenting.

A person experiencing any sort of marginalization can't leave their home without feeling their distance from the mainstream and the many subtle forms of rejection that come with that difference. Discrimination is a form of suffering that wears down the human spirit, making it challenging to live vitally.

If you are suffering from any form of institutionally enforced marginalization, from a mind-body-spirit perspective, please know that I understand, deeply, how even if you follow my formulas to soothe, it's incredibly difficult to live from a place of spirit. While there are many brave souls who have found ways to remain self-loving and vibrant in the face of discrimination (find them and learn from them!), it's one of the worst forms of suffering I see as a therapist, and I send you a little extra love and courage as you find ways to transcend it and live from a place of a core being.

MY FAVORITE SPIRIT-BOOSTING TECHNIQUE OF ALL:
COMPASSION

We've talked about the role beliefs play in our reality, and we've talked about digging deep and seeing where you can empower, vitalize, and lift your beliefs about how the world works and your value in it. Additionally, we've talked about giving special attention to your beliefs about the reality of human suffering and what we're meant to do with it. Here's one more spirit-boosting technique that, I will argue, lays at the heart of spiritual strength and resilience. It's my favorite emotional health technique, and I try to use it often.

We've already talked about the nature of the mind. The mind loves to judge. It loves to say what is good and what is bad and what should be and what shouldn't be. And no matter how much you meditate, get counseling, distract, and do all of the things in this book, the mind will never stop judging. It's a hardwired feature of our humanness, and we simply need to accept it. But just as the mind judges, the spirit experiences compassion. For every single life experience that we judge with our minds, we can equally access compassion with our spirits. And it is extremely important to note that compassion includes both self-compassion and other-compassion.

The good news is, you don't have to get rid of your judgments. Most of us can't! At least not authentically. But every time you catch a big smelly judgment, see if you can partner it with both self-compassion and other-compassion.

Let's start with a very common example. In all of my training as a psychologist, nothing prepared me for how often I would hear the following (usually from women):

"Dr. Heidi, I know I'm pleasant and congenial in here. But you would not recognize me at home with my husband. Time after time, we both come home from a long day at work and I tend to the children and start dinner and put in a load of laundry, and he immediately sits on the couch and plays on his phone. And Heidi, when this happens, I become hard inside and I seethe with resentment.

I've asked for help, and he might help a little bit, but it doesn't take long before he's back on the couch. So I stomp around and make biting comments. Eventually I lose it and yell at him like a raging looney. I don't recognize myself when this happens and then I feel ashamed. I promise, I am light and friendly with all other people! But with the man I'm supposed to love above all others, I feel judgment and anger. And I feel shame toward myself."

Now, if you think I'm going to gloss over this complex situation with, "Just find some compassion in your heart," you're wrong. But I do think, before my client is going to find an effective way to manage this situation, she needs to identify all the layers of judgment and see where she can partner those judgments with compassion.

And here's where it gets a bit tricky, because you may think her judgment is against her husband. But she actually has more judgment against herself for getting angry. *For compassion to work, we have to identify and counter both the judgment against ourselves and the judgment against others.*

Let's continue. With my client, I might ask her, "Tell me, in what ways are you judging yourself in this scenario?" It's easy to see that she is judging herself for becoming so angry and not knowing what to do with her anger.

So I start there. I ask my client, "If a friend told you she felt frazzled and overwhelmed managing the bulk of her family's domestic tasks, what would you think?" Inevitably, my client will say that she would have compassion for how hard it is to feel alone with so many responsibilities. I then ask my client to apply that compassion to herself. *Of course* she gets angry when she feels overburdened and unsupported. That is her fight response trying to give her the power to change things. Her anger is understandable, human, and deserving of compassion.

Only when I am fully convinced that my client feels some self-compassion, can we turn toward the other person. (I have no way of proving this, but I personally believe self-compassion has to happen first in order for other-compassion to be effective and authentic.)

So after my client gives herself a little compassion for feeling rightfully overwhelmed and angry, we can focus on her husband. Her mind judges him for not helping and for ignoring his family. But what about her spirit? Does it have compassion for him? Usually I hear something along the lines of, "Yes. He is tired at the end of the day and needs a break before he can function. And he does help when asked. And he truly seems wired differently from me. It's like his brain doesn't register the details of what needs to be done like mine does. And though this is frustrating, I also think he's doing the best he can."

Okay, now we're there. My client has judgment for her anger, but also compassion for her anger. She has judgment against her husband, but equal compassion for their differences. This does not mean the problem is solved and my client will never be angry again. But partnering judgment with compassion does put my client in a more balanced place emotionally, and from there we can effectively brainstorm my client's best course of action.

In some cases that means trying different ways of communicating. Sometimes that means building tolerance for the differences between a client and their spouse. Sometimes it might mean ending a relationship. The solution is not the focus here.

The point is, when we get swept up into our judgments, it becomes impossible to soothe our emotions or access satisfying solutions to our problems. When we act solely from a place of judgment, we are likely to act rashly and ineffectively. We do not need to get rid of our judgments, but by partnering the judgments of the mind with the compassion of the spirit—both toward ourselves and others—we become more even-keeled and, hopefully, more effective in our resolution-seeking behaviors.

Let's examine an even pithier example of this. Eric was the owner of a gas station/convenience store in a small and friendly community. He knew many of the clients who passed through his shop, and he genuinely enjoyed working the cash register and engaging with customers. Eric had owned his business his entire adult life and was nearing retirement.

One slow afternoon, two young adult men whom Eric didn't recognize came into the shop. Right away, they started acting suspiciously, mumbling to each other and looking around the shop as though surveying it. Then, quite suddenly, one of the men pulled out a gun and pointed it at Eric while the other blocked the door. Eric was commanded to open the cash register and hand over the money, which he did without argument. When the gunman took the cash, he hit Eric in the head with the gun, telling him he'd better not contact the police.

Eric healed from the injury of the blow, and he was able to return to work shortly after this incident. However, everything changed for Eric after the robbery. He found himself scrutinizing everyone who came into the store, especially if he didn't know them. He struggled to feel safe or comfortable at work, and he found himself exhausted at the end of each shift, presumably from being in a state of hyperalert all day.

Even worse, Eric found himself replaying the assault in his head. He would become angry with himself for not instantly recognizing that the men were planning on robbing him. He wished he would have fought back, rather than handing over the money. He felt angry that people were capable of taking advantage of others the way his two assailants had, and he found himself wishing ill things on these men, which wasn't like Eric.

Eric's healing from this traumatic incident was multifaceted. Because his system was constantly on high alert, Eric needed to learn and actively practice a wide variety of body-soothing techniques. We also needed to address the newfound fears created by the robbery. Finding techniques to effectively soothe those fears took time. But Eric's true healing came when we explored his judgments of the situation and partnered them with compassion.

Eric had many judgments toward himself. He believed he should have handled things differently. He believed he should have foreseen the robbery and acted sooner. With time, Eric was able to partner these judgments with compassion. He could see that it was actually a testament to his character that he gave these men the benefit of the doubt when they came in. He could also see that his body very naturally and healthily chose a high-arousal freeze response over a fight response. He realized, in time, that this was probably the best response for this particular situation, and it is the one he would have chosen for anyone else, had they been in his place.

After Eric cultivated self-compassion, we were able to turn toward other-compassion. Eric's judgment of the two men was that they were bad people who took advantage of Eric. And this judgment is fair to have—there was no need to try to change it. But Eric was equally able to find compassion for the two men. They clearly lacked life skills, values, and well-being if holding up convenience stores was how they were getting by. Eric found himself feeling blessed to have a community of people to turn to for support after the assault. He was able to surround himself with love. The two men who robbed him, however, were likely rarely free from the feelings of violence and chaos they inflicted on Eric that day, and this made Eric sad for them.

When Eric began partnering his judgments with compassion, both toward himself and his perpetrators, Eric truly started feeling "like his old self" again. Compassion filled him with the resilience he initially lost. But getting to a place of compassion needed to happen authentically. And it did require soothing the body and the mind before there was room for the deeper work of the spirit.

Judgment and compassion are like yin and yang. We need both. But, in so many situations, we live from one or the other. When you are struggling, see if you can find your judgments and partner them with compassion. Make sure you're evaluating both your judgment toward yourself and your judgment toward others. And remember, blind compassion without judgment can arguably be as hazardous as blind judgment without compassion. In difficult situations, look for both. When you've identified your judgments and compassion, both your mind and your spirit can engage as equals in figuring out how you'd like to navigate challenges.

A SUMMARY OF SPIRIT

Our spirit is comprised of our deepest beliefs about how the world works and our value in that world. To lift your spirit, dig into your collection of beliefs and find the brightest, strongest beliefs (that you actually believe) and bring them to the forefront of your awareness over and over and over (and over) again. In particular, look at your beliefs about the purpose of suffering and what you believe we humans should do with the reality of this. Also, don't forget to identify the judgments of your mind, and partner them with the compassion of your spirit. We need both.

CHAPTER 10

■ ■ ■

WHAT DO WE DO FOR
LIFE'S REALLY TOUGH STUFF?

We all encounter situations that are bigger than day-to-day stressors. For example, emotionally recovering from a trauma is a lot bigger fish to fry than finishing your work emails for the day. Or dealing with the death of a loved one requires more tender, loving care than gaining 10 pounds and feeling anxious about weight. So I would like to explore how to self-counsel when you hit something intense emotionally. This is the formula for the big stuff. For the stuff we can't change or alter with action. It requires you to stop the momentum of your life and take some time to contemplate and explore internally, and it looks like this:

1. *STOP.* This is such a hard step when you're swept up into a crappy emotion. But it's also the most important. When you are in a really tough emotional place, step one is to bring everything to a complete halt and find a bit of privacy to process your experience.

2. *Name your emotions.* When a child raises her hand in class and gets ignored, she'll only raise it higher and start bouncing up and down. When an emotion wants your attention and gets ignored, it will only turn up the volume and start pestering you until you acknowledge it. Do that for the tough stuff. It doesn't take long. Simply finish this sentence: "Wow, do I ever feel _____."

3. *Soothe the body.* As much as you are able, soften your breath, soften your muscles, unclench your jaw, relax your belly. Use your imagination to soften your energy. Engage in the reactive body-soothing techniques explored in Chapter 6. Remove as much physical tension as possible.

4. *Find the fear or fears underneath the emotions and softly dialogue with them.* Remember, it can be challenging to find the fears underneath a negative emotional experience, but there is always some sort of fear at the root. Take some time to explore what yours might be. Then review the techniques explored in the mind-soothing chapters of this book and see which fears can be quieted, even if only a little bit. Resist the temptation to say things like, "I shouldn't fear that," or "What is wrong with me for feeling so fearful?" Study your fears and engage with them as though they are large-eyed whimpering puppies.

5. *Dig deep and find your best beliefs.* You probably have many perfectly valid beliefs about your situation that are negative in nature, but there's a good chance you're forgetting a few empowering beliefs that could help you. What positive beliefs about yourself, your worth, your resources, your friends and family, your resilience, your spirituality, are you forgetting? What are the best beliefs you can access, no matter how dire the situation? Ignite your most vital beliefs and repeatedly remind yourself of these.

6. *Go back to the beginning and do it all again*, and again, and again, until you start to feel a shift. Some situations will take longer than others, but soothing will eventually take hold if you stick with it, I promise.

A FEW EXAMPLES ...

I'm going to use one personal example that's on the lighter end, a client situation that is more intense, and a global concern that we're all dealing with. Here's the lighter, personal one.

Psychologists, some are surprised to learn, don't earn very impressive salaries. I'm blessed to have an amazing job and paid bills, but there is often little (and sometimes nothing) left over. As many Americans can relate, money has been both a stressor and a fear for my entire adult life.

Every time a bill arrives, I immediately feel anxious. My chest tightens, my stomach flip flops and my mind starts fluttering about "How am I going to pay for X?" and "Will there be enough for Y?" Then I personalize my situation by thinking about friends who just went on an expensive vacation or purchased a new car or seem to always be wearing something new and shiny.

After that, I catastrophize by wondering about what will happen if something really big occurs, like a health issue. And will I ever be able to retire? And even if I can't retire, will anyone want to see a 90-year-old therapist? Will I be a dried-up, 90-year-old therapist with no money or friends or family? Am I doing something wrong that money is so hard? And what is wrong with the world that money is so hard? As long as I'm on a roll, how come life is so hard? And while we're at it, how come people die? And how will I die? Will I choke when I'm eating my protein, good fat, and high-fiber carbs? Will someone hate this book and come to kill me? Will I be a 90-year-old therapist choking on food and being murdered? Whaaaaaaaaaa!

As you can see, I've worked myself into an anxious, irritated, depressive fit—all spawned by a $65 bill for Wi-Fi (which is, for the record, a ridiculous price to pay for internet access...).

So how do I deal with this from a mind-body-spirit perspective? First, I STOP. And believe it or not, that's the hardest part. It's so much easier just to get swept up into my internal frenzy than it is to put a wrench in it. To stop, I actually have to scream this in my head and see the word reverberate through my mind. I then briefly state, "Wow, do I ever feel anxious."

Next, I start the body-soothing process. I take a deep breath. I put my hand to my chest. If I'm home, I grab a small handful of nuts. I walk around for a little bit.

Then I find the fear. My fear is that I will never have enough money to live my life fully. This fear is partly rational, partly irrational, but that doesn't matter, because fears need to be soothed whether they're real or imaginary. So I start with one or two mind-soothing techniques. "Shhhhhhhhh. Light and easy, Heidi. Light and easy." Then I go back to body soothing by putting both feet firmly on the ground and breathing in. Then, I go back to a mind-soothing technique—I shift my inner voice to a nurturing tone: "Heidi, you've got this. You're okay. You're safe. You will figure this out."

I then return to body soothing. This time, I soften my breath and look to the horizon. Here I might also scan my body and soften the muscles that are unconsciously tense (usually the jaw and shoulders for me).

Next, I return to mind soothing. For this example, I'm drawn toward the "What do I trust?" technique. I trust that I have always figured out money in the past. I trust that I always have the skills to make money some way, somehow. I trust that I can live simply and spend less. I trust that part of my money problems are in my head, and I have all that I need. I trust that there are rewards to my financial situation, such as appreciation for small pleasures and mindfulness of what I consume.

Okay, it's taken a few minutes, but I'm actually starting to feel better. Now it's time to get to the level of the spirit. What belief about money is dragging me down right now? It's the belief that I won't ever have enough. This belief plagues many of us. So what belief that I actually believe can be summoned instead of the belief that there is never enough? Well, I believe, when I really stop and think about it, that I actually *do* have enough, but my fear blinds me to this. And I have the spiritual belief that the universe often provides when you least expect it. I just lose sight of these beliefs sometimes.

Ahhhh, I have arrived. I haven't changed the fact that I have my Wi-Fi bill to pay, and I haven't changed my income in that moment, but I have reoriented so that rather than living from a place of fear, I am living from a place of a calm body, a soothed mind, and a strong spirit. And from here, I am more likely to make wise choices about spending, as well as draw in more unexpected ways to handle my fear.

Let's move on to a more serious client example. Maggie, a woman in her early 30s, experienced a traumatic event as a teenager. Her best friend's father, a respected and successful man whom she looked up to, sexually assaulted her at the age of 18. Maggie had gone to visit her friend at her home, but everyone was gone except her friend's father. He invited her inside and offered her an alcoholic beverage, stating that this was a special "adult" celebration of her recent high school graduation.

This was extremely uncomfortable for Maggie, but also strangely thrilling. She equally wanted to leave and stay. But after one beverage, her friend's father started kissing and touching her, eventually having his way with her. Maggie was terrified. She wanted to get away, but she also didn't have the strength to tell this man no. She had always sought to gain the approval of adults her entire life, and she had no experience saying no and defending herself in this way. She also felt like she was responsible for what was happening since she had accepted his offer of a drink, and she suddenly wondered if she had been leading him on all these years.

Maggie felt frozen, ashamed, and humiliated. She felt like this man saw her as worthless and trashy, since he was willing to use her in this way. She also thought he must be seeing something everyone else saw in her, as well.

Afterward, Maggie didn't tell anyone because she knew her friend would be horrified, and Maggie feared the loss of their friendship. Maggie also feared that if the man's wife knew, it would cause a divorce and then everyone would hate and blame Maggie for being a homewrecker. As if that weren't enough, Maggie also didn't want her own parents to learn about the encounter. She knew this would break their hearts, and she feared that they would view her differently.

If you met Maggie, you would never guess that she was suffering from this experience. She had graduated from college and was in the throes of a lucrative career when I met her. She had friends and a calendar full of activities. But underneath, Maggie felt lonely. She felt like, if others were to get too close to her, they would see her as her friend's father saw her. Tainted. Not worthy of respect. Insignificant.

Maggie didn't date. On occasion, she would drink too much at a party and experience a casual physical encounter, but these were unsatisfying and only fueled her belief that men found no value in her beyond sex. Maggie's primary stress response was freeze. She was active and social, but a part of her remained hidden and stagnant inside. And when she was alone, Maggie would feel depressed.

Maggie worked hard in her therapy sessions, but when she was on her own, I asked her to follow my formula as best as she was able and report back to me. Here's an example of Maggie's process:

Step 1—Stop. When Maggie was home and feeling blue, she would turn off her TV and sit on her couch for a few moments.

Step 2— Name the emotion. Maggie would take a deep breath and say aloud, "I'm feeling confused and overwhelmed and lost and depressed and lonely and without hope."

Step 3— Soften the body. For Maggie, in her darker moments, everything would feel heavy and numb. Her belly would knot up. Her chest felt hollow and dark. Her muscles and mind felt sluggish. For Maggie, this step wasn't so much about softening, but rather about sending some mental warmth to her entire body. She would imagine a soothing light washing through her and trying to help her.

Step 4—Find the fear. Maggie had many fears as a result of her trauma. Some of these fears she was able to identify. Some required my help as a psychologist. Maggie was afraid that she deserved the treatment she received from her friend's father. She feared that if she let any man get close, he would see that she was worthless and treat her in the same way. She feared that she was fundamentally weak. She feared she was a bad friend to her friend. She feared her story being discovered and everyone seeing her as a tramp. She feared that her pain would never go away and that she would never be "normal," let alone happy.

Because Maggie had so many fears, I suggested that she pick the one that felt the most pressing and see if she could gently attend to it. Maggie worked on all of her fears over time, but the one that really caused her the most pain was the fear that she had somehow caused the assault that she experienced (this is a common fear for those who experience any sort of abuse). And this fear was not easy for Maggie to soothe. Over time, she learned that challenging the fear was a good place to start: "Maggie, you were a teenager and he was a fully grown adult who had been a father figure to you. He took advantage of that. You did not ask for sexual assault, you asked for approval, and that is a perfectly normal thing for a teen to want from an adult!" From there, Maggie would try some nurturing inner self-talk: "Shhhh. You've got this. You're safe now, Maggie. You're going to be okay."

Step 5—Access vital beliefs. Maggie had to spend quite a bit of time both soothing and rallying against her fear. This process did not produce instant results for her, but if she was able to stay with the fear-soothing long enough, she would eventually start to feel a shift. And then Maggie would ask herself, "What is the best belief I can access right now?" She received a different response from her spirit every time, but usually it was something along the lines of, "You have value and you will heal." She also found comfort in the belief of, "Some men take advantage of women, but most men don't." And she would practice saying these beliefs over and over until she felt her resilience growing.

Through her own work and with counseling, Maggie truly did heal. That doesn't mean she stopped being triggered by the memory of her experience. But with time and persistence, Maggie became more and more skilled at identifying what fears were present at any given time and what techniques worked with those fears.

Eventually, Maggie said she didn't need to evaluate and soothe her fears anymore. She could just skip to the spirit part and remind herself of her best beliefs, which is that she is valued, and most people are good. (Maggie, if you're reading this you might not recognize yourself, because I have altered the details for your privacy. But please know you did amazing work, and your healing inspired and moved me.)

Let's shift gears and tackle a mounting universal fear. Regardless of your politics or religious beliefs, we are all living in a time where we experience fears about the future of the planet and humanity. I have a proliferation of clients coming to therapy with depression or anxiety or anger, not due to personal stressors, but due to the state of the world. Because we feel so helpless about what's happening globally, this fear is incredibly challenging to navigate psychologically. So what do we do?

Start by stopping. When you catch your "I'm scared for the planet" or "I'm scared for humanity" malaise, see if you can take a moment to just stop.

Next take a moment to name your emotions. "Phooey, do I ever feel _____."

Next, choose a body-soothing technique. Breathe. Place your hand to your chest.

Next, name your fears. Perhaps you fear that the world will end. Maybe you fear the actions of people in power. Maybe you fear for the suffering of people and animals. Maybe you fear that things will only continue to get worse. These fears are likely a combination of rational and irrational. It doesn't matter; they all need soothing.

Next, implement a mind-soothing technique. Perhaps start with some comforting, "Shhhhhh's." Remember, we're not trying to solve the problem, we're trying to get to an emotional place where we can effectively navigate the world with resilience rather than just reacting to the world from a place of fear.

Next, go back to the body-soothing techniques. Change your temperature with a mug of green tea. Eat some cheese and a few slices of apple with almond butter.

Then go back to the mind-soothing techniques. Perhaps ask yourself, "Who do I want to be in this world?" Follow that with, "What do I trust?" Perhaps try out, "What thought soothes me a little bit?"

When fear begins to dissipate in intensity and you feel ready, examine your deepest beliefs about the world, and find the most vital ones. Do you believe that the experiences of our planet have a greater purpose? Do you believe what's happening has the potential to change over time? Do you believe that even though there are ways where it looks like we're devolving as a species, that there are also ways that we are evolving? Do you believe humans have the ability to solve the problems they created? Do you believe it's okay to be concerned about the world, but also to take mental breaks from being concerned? Do you believe that there are things you can do that will have a positive impact?

This part is deeply personal work, and the beliefs that work for one might not for another. But the goal is the same for everyone in all situations: Find your most energizing beliefs and activate them.

As an added note, some people fear that if they try to soothe their fears about the world, they will then become numb, apathetic, or worse, delusional, about world problems and lose touch with reality. This simply isn't true. Finding your best beliefs about a situation helps you approach life with resilience and hope so that you may better impact the world in a meaningful way.

A BRIEF SUMMARY

When you encounter something really challenging, carve out some time and use the following formula. *Stop. Name your emotions. Soothe your body. Find your fears and soothe your mind. Access the best beliefs of your spirit.* Do this over and over again. It's not easy, but this is how we heal and become resilient.

BONUS CHAPTER:
USING THE MIND-BODY-SPIRIT
IN DECISION-MAKING

Having awareness of the body, mind, and spirit can be surprisingly helpful for making challenging decisions. When you're at a fork in the road and you just can't choose which direction to go, the tendency is to turn to the mind for a response. And the mind will always do the same darn thing—it lists the pros and cons of its options. It tells you what you need to, have to, got to, should do. It judges anything and everything. It finds all the possible ways things could go wrong or get screwed up.

The mind is rarely helpful when it comes to tough decisions. So we remain confused. We ping and we pong and we pong and we ping, back and forth, forth and back. Do I fight through this job or find a new one? Do I go back to school or not? Do I challenge this situation or do I ignore it? Do I stay in this relationship or leave it? Do I save for the future or live in the moment?

In order to involve the mind, the body, and the spirit in decision-making, we listen to input from all three equally. I'll start with a very simple example, something I think we can all relate to: someone bringing sweets to the office after we've just eaten a sizeable lunch. Grrr-argh, how a part of us desperately wants those chocolate-covered, no-bake peanut butter balls with their sweet and gooey goodness! But another part of us says, "I shouldn't eat that; I just had lunch." Making decisions like this can be easier if you call in the troops: mind, body, and spirit.

Here's how it works. I take five seconds and I hold the image of a chocolate covered, peanut butter ball in my being. Then I notice the response of my body. I notice that my mouth starts to salivate and I get a tingling feeling thinking about the first bite. Body says, "Yes, please, bring on the goodies!!" Then I turn to the mind. The mind says, "You shouldn't eat that, you just had lunch, you big oinker." (The stupid mind almost always says no to the fun stuff.) Then I turn to the spirit by focusing on the energy right in the center of my heart, and I'm quiet for just a moment.

And although it's subtle, I notice a slight sense of constriction. Spirit says, "Not today—resting and digesting actually feels better than eating more." I tally the votes, and I have one yes and two no's. No chocolate-covered, no-bake peanut butter ball for me today, but, dear body, maybe next time!

Can you see the benefit of bringing in three voters for tough decisions? Depending on the situation, most of us tend toward a two-party system. When it comes to eating and drinking, our bodies say one thing and our minds say another. When it comes to major life decisions, our minds say one thing and our hearts say another. Calling in a third voice adds more clarity.

Let me give you a more nuanced and personal example. There was a time in my life where I was at a very formidable fork in the road. It's a long story, but I spent a period of time working as a motor-coach driver in Alaska. It was a fantastic job, as it allowed me to travel and explore the entire state. After I dropped off tourists at their destinations, I was able to don my backpack and hike to my heart's content, just as long as I was showered and ready to pick up passengers again the next day.

This was a summertime job only, and as I neared the end of the season, I received a compelling offer to drive motor coaches for another tour company that arranged cross-country trips and operated year-round. My life would have been very adventurous, providing tours and transportation to an outdoorsy clientele throughout the nation. This was a job that appealed to my wanderlust, as well as my desire to live off the beaten path.

And yet …

While it seemed a distant dream, I also had developed niggling ideas of going back to school for psychology. I wasn't sure, at the time, what that entailed or whether it was even possible. School would require financing I didn't have and time I didn't want to sacrifice. And I would need to procure some sort of steady day job and a place to live. All of this was a far cry from a free-spirited life of bus driving and camping.

List after list of pros and cons didn't clarify. One path seemed exciting. The other would develop a career that while not as adventurous, would give me a sense of safety, purpose, and direction. One path would allow travel and meeting new people. The other path would challenge me intellectually.

The mind-body-spirit technique looked like this. I held the option of becoming a full-time motor-coach driver in my being for a few moments and then noticed, "What does my body say?" It took a few moments, but I noticed a slight tightening in my belly and a very subtle, almost unobservable, feeling of tension. Then I turned toward the mind. This instrument was predictably useless. It just kept going back and forth—yes, no, maybe so. Then I focused on the center of my body, near my heart, looking for a sense of expansion or constriction. And honestly, I couldn't tell. So here's the tally, body says no, mind and spirit—undecided.

Next, I held the option of returning to school in my being. I tuned into my body and it felt a bit numb. Nothing tightened, as it did with the motor-coach position, but nothing lightened or softened either. When I turned to the mind, that wasn't any help. It just went back and forth between, "Driving would be unique" to "Becoming a psychologist would be a smart thing for you to do." Then I turned inward, and here's where the clarity came. When I thought of becoming a psychologist, something in me lightened and felt just a tiny bit easier. It wasn't overwhelming, but I definitely felt an ease of sorts when I contemplated this.

So here was the tally: body neutral, mind undecided, spirit yes. Overall, when the votes were compared, the motor coach job was neutral to no, and the psychologist path was neutral to yes. I had my direction, even if it was a blurry one. And since it came from the consensus of mind, body, and spirit, I felt strongly about the direction I chose, even though it was hard to let go of the alternative route.

As you can see from that example, this isn't a perfect, crystal-clear process. Initially, it takes time and practice to tune into the responses of the body and the spirit, but over time, it becomes more and more natural, I promise. Also, sometimes the cues from the body and spirit are fairly subtle and challenging to interpret. But, at the end of the day, using the mind, the body, and the spirit when making difficult decisions provides you with more data and information, and when you do land on an answer, you'll feel more confident in your choice.

CONCLUSION

That was it—that's my book. I sincerely hope that you have a different conceptualization of emotions now than you did 158 pages ago. I hope you feel like you can tell your family and friends what emotions are, where they come from, why we have them, and some ideas about what we do with them. I also hope that you've dog-eared a few of these pages to begin implementing the techniques immediately. I want you to be breathing softly and fully, right now in this very moment. I want the voice in your head, no matter what it's thinking, to be expressing those thoughts in a nurturing way. And somewhere, deep inside of you, I hope your spirit is optimistic that it will start peeking out from underneath those mind-driven need-to-have-to-got-to-shoulds.

And please, for the love of cat film festivals, remind yourself that every time you have a negative emotion, it is your body and mind and spirit's way of expressing the most natural feeling in the world, one that we experience much of our day: *fear*. But now we also know that fear doesn't need to be feared as much as we think it does. It just needs to be … are you ready for the grand finale here? … SOOTHED.

Soothe the body to soothe the mind. Soothe the mind to ignite the spirit. My work here is done. Anyone got a pat of butter I can eat or a dry body brush I can use? Otherwise, I'm going for a glass of wine.

With Love,
Heidi Kopacek

Made in the USA
Monee, IL
16 March 2022

92977298R00094